Preface

As if to illustrate how rapidly events are lost to memory, one person after viewing the galley proof of this book, with attendant "oooh's" and "aaah's" of pleasure, asked what the Northern Pacific Railway was! The Northern Pacific Railway, along with the Great Northern and the Chicago, Burlington, and Quincy, was merged into the Burlington Northern in 1970.

Warren McGee and Ronald Nixon have preserved the Northern Pacific Railway as no one else. Their jobs with the NP and the railroads use of them as official photographers, gave them unusually fine photographic opportunities. These photographs convey the expanse and beauty of the environment which the NP traversed and served as well as the majestic power of the iron horses in their super, yet final years of glory. The photo story concludes with the transition into the first generation diesel power age. Steam power is allowed to fade off in its glory, its dignity not sullied by scrapping scenes.

The fine quality eighty pound non-glare matte enamel paper was specifically chosen to enhance enjoyment of these large, detailed photographic moments in history by eliminating page glare.

The book is organized by locomotive type, except the special chapter on the Yellowstone Park Line, and within chapters generally chronologically so that the reader can follow the locomotive type, sometimes a specific locomotive, from its earliest years noting changes through the years.

Of special help to researchers are the indexes. The locomotive index is organized by locomotive type with specific locomotives indexed numerically making it easy to locate pictures desired. In some instances, a locomotive is indexed that is not visible in the particular photograph, but which was at the scene. This is done to aid modelers and historians endeavoring to accurately recreate specific scenes or periods with accurate representation of equipment assigned in the location at the time.

The map indexes provide a quick and simple method to find photographs of specific areas and locations. The map indexes are bound into the book and in addition are printed on the inside of the dustcover to alleviate the nuisance of repeated page flipping to the bound-in maps. Just lay the dustjacket out flat and reference and locate desired scenes.

Additional information provided for your enjoyment includes a roster of remaining NP steam locomotives and their locations, train number and name schedule covering trains pictured, NP lettering stencil drawings, etc.

Richard Green has collected Northern Pacific memorabilia second to none. His extensive collection of photographs by McGee and Nixon was the source for the outstanding scenes he selected for this book. These photographs include the regular operations of the day, rare photographs taken at remote locations which took years to arrange, and operations such as double-heading of Challengers (forbidden by the rules the photographer tells us in the captions) and the use of articulated locomotives on high speed passenger trains, an unusual event for any railroad except the Northern Pacific as author Green shows us here.

Errata: Page 46 date should read 7-30-51.

This page: Train No. 26 with NP 6511 and eleven cars at East Auburn, Washington on 12-26-52. *W.R. McGee*

Previous page: Train No. 4 with NP 2265 arriving at Auburn, Washington on 5-16-46. *R.V. Nixon*

Front end paper: NP 2661 and the eleven car North Coast Limited departing St. Paul, Minnesota on 5-17-40. *W.R. McGee*

Rear end paper: NP 5107 and the second section of the North Coast Limited (pullman section) leaving Livingston, Montana on 6-14-37. *W.R. McGee*

THE
NORTHERN PACIFIC
RAILWAY

OF McGEE AND NIXON

Classic photographs of equipment and environment during the 1930-1955 period

By RICHARD GREEN

NORTHWEST SHORT LINE
Seattle, Washington

Dedication

To my wife Carol, for her encouragement and assistance.

Acknowledgments

The guidance in this book has come from many individuals. I would like to thank the following for their generous assistance.

First and foremost are Warren McGee and Ron Nixon. Without their photos, important data, and stories, this book would not have been possible. They have taken a lot of their time to answer my many questions.

Mike Gelhaus for his special help in technical information, insights on NP passenger trains, and useful suggestions.

I would also like to thank the following individuals: Aram Langhans, Yolande Maxwell, Norm Mikelson, and Larry Richards.

To all, thank you very much!

Published by NorthWest Short Line
Box 423, Seattle, Washington 98111-0423 USA
SAN 693-2037

Copyright 1985 by Richard Green

Book Concept by F. Raoul Martin and Scott Law
Book Design and Typography by Scott Law Design
Lithography by Sunrise Printing, Seattle
Manufactured in the United States of America

Library of Congress Number 85-61050
ISBN 0-915370-03-4

At right: Train No. 3 with NP 1635 and 2193 crosses Montana's Marent Trestle in June of 1933. *R. V. Nixon*

Main Street of the Northwest

NORTHERN PACIFIC
YELLOWSTONE PARK LINE

PASSENGER
SCHEDULES

NORTH COAST
Limited

Contents

Introduction
Train Number Schedule

Locomotive Index
Maps - Line and Photograph Locations

Introduction

I am excited about bringing you some of the finest Northern Pacific action photos that I have ever seen. In planning this book, emphasis was put on scenes which depicted the trains in their native surroundings and the majestic scenery through which they operated. This book is a result of collecting information and photos for many years, and feeling that it's important to share this information with others. Most of all, it is intended as a tribute to the exceptional motive power of the Northern Pacific and is dedicated to its many fans.

This book features the outstanding camera work of Warren McGee and Ron Nixon, two of the NP's finest photographers. Many railroads hired professional photographers, but the NP relied on its own employees. This left the railroad to be documented by those who knew it best, those who where a living, working part of it. The photography of McGee and Nixon speaks for itself, every photo as fine a piece of work as any professional could have produced. This book exhibits but a small portion of their vast collections. Without photographers like Warren and Ron, the locomotives of the NP would be just an unclear memory. Their accomplishments are remarkable considering the isolated areas at which many of these photos were taken. Many of the scenes were captured only after hiking miles through terrible weather conditions. The infrequency of trains on the NP didn't help either. Both Warren and Ron are best known for the work they did in their home state of Montana, so these photos are emphasized here.

The photos I have selected for this book are mainly confined to those taken between the years of 1930 to 1955. This is the period I consider to be the glory years on the NP, with the super powered steam locomotives and the very interesting early diesels. No attempt was made to show all the different power that operated on the railroad. The book focuses on steam action, as this is how I would like best to remember the NP.

There is no formal text, the captions serve as the informational source. I have relied heavily on personal stories and opinions by the two photographers to add a human touch to the book, rather than just facts and figures. Other railroad books have frustrated me in the past by omitting locations or dates on some of the photos. I've made every effort to see that each photo in this book has both. Hopefully this should prove useful to both historian and modeler alike.

Each chapter focuses on a particular locomotive wheel classification. After each introductory page, the locomotive class is followed chronologically as much as possible, though sometimes not completely, due to size and space limitations. In some cases, certain locomotives are shown throughout the class section in various stages of development, from first run to near retirement.

May these photos bring you hours of enjoyment, as they have me.

Dick Green
January 1985

No. 1—Daily—West Example of Daily Service		Miles	Detailed schedules between Chicago and Seattle - Tacoma - Portland on pages 8 to 13	No. 2—Daily—East Example of Daily Service	
			Central Time		
Sunday	**11 00 pm**	0	Lv..CHICAGO (C. B. & Q.)..Ar.	7 50 am	Wednesday
Monday	8 40 am	431	Lv.ST. PAUL, via N. P. Ry..Ar.	**10 00 pm**	Tuesday
"	9 15 am	10	Lv.....MINNEAPOLIS.....Ar.	9 27 pm	"
Monday	7 30 am	0	Lv.......DULUTH.......Ar.	**10 50 pm**	Tuesday
"	7 45 am	4	Lv.....SUPERIOR.......Ar.	10 34 pm	"
Monday	**2 28 pm**	252	Ar........Fargo........Ar.	**4 11 pm**	Tuesday
"	**4 50 pm**	344	Ar.......Jamestown......Lv.	2 15 pm	"
"	**7 05 pm**	446	Ar........Bismarck.......Lv.	12 20 pm	"
			Mountain Time		
"	**6 30 pm**	451	Ar........Mandan......Ar.	10 55 am	"
"	**8 57 pm**	551	Ar........Dickinson......Lv.	8 40 am	"
"	**11 30 pm**	657	Ar.......Glendive......Lv.	6 10 am	"
Tuesday	1 27 am	736	Ar.......Miles City......Lv.	4 18 am	"
"	2 35 am	781	Ar.......Forsyth......Lv.	3 15 am	"
"	5 00 am	883	Ar.......Billings......Lv.	1 00 am	"
"	a 9 15 am	59	Ar......Red Lodge......Lv.	a 4 45 pm	Monday
"	7 50 am	999	Ar.......Livingston......Lv.	10 35 pm	"
Tuesday	c10 30 am	1053	Ar.......Gardiner......Lv.	c 7 45 pm	....
Tuesday	11 45 am	1122	Ar.......Helena.......Lv.	6 20 pm	Monday
"	**12 15 pm**	1119	Ar.......Butte.......Lv.	6 30 pm	"
"	**3 05 pm**	1238	Ar.......Missoula.......Lv.	3 45 pm	"
			Pacific Time		
"	d **7 41 pm**	1456	Ar.........Athol........Lv.	d 9 26 am	"
			Farragut		
"	**8 35 pm**	1496	Ar........Spokane.......Lv.	8 40 am	"
Wednesday	12 13 am	1641	Ar...Pasco via N. P. Ry...Lv.	5 02 am	"
"	2 25 am	1731	Ar........YAKIMA.......Lv.	3 10 am	"
"	3 31 am	1768	Ar...ELLENSBURG....Lv.	2 00 am	"
"	7 30 am	1892	Ar.......SEATTLE.......Lv.	**10 30 pm**	Sunday
"	7 30 am	1889	Ar.......TACOMA.......Lv.	10 10 pm	"

Spokane-Portland					
Tuesday	**9 00 pm**	0	Lv...Spokane (N. P. Ry.)..Ar.	8 15 am	Monday
Wednesday	1 50 am	147	Lv..Pasco (S. P. & S. Ry.)..Ar.	2 40 am	Monday
"	7 35 am	377	Ar.......Portland.......Lv. via S. P. & S. Ry.	8 45 pm	Sunday

California Via Puget Sound

458 Daily		**408** Daily		**402** Daily		Pacific Time	**401** Daily		**407** Daily	
We.	**3 50**	We.	**12 01**	We.	**11 30**	Lv....Seattle....Ar.	6 45	Su.	**4 35**	Su.
We.	**5 05**	We.	**12 57**	Th.	1 00	Lv....Tacoma....Ar.	5 00	Su.	**3 25**	Su.
We.	**8 50**	We.	**4 35**	Th.	6 45	Ar....Portland....Lv.	11 30	Sa.	**12 01**	Su.

15 Daily		**11** Daily		**19** Daily		**Southern Pacific**	**20** Daily		**12** Daily	
We.	**9 50**	We.	**4 50**	Th.	8 15	Lv....Portland....Ar.	**9 50**	Sa.	**11 30**	Su.
Th.	**10 42**	Th.	10 50	Fri.	7 45	Ar..Oakland Pier..Lv.	8 45	Fri.	**5 35**	Sa.
Th.	**11 10**	Th.	11 20	Fri.	8 20	Ar..San Francisco..Lv.	8 00	Fri.	**5 00**	Sa.
Fr.	8 45	Th.	9 55	Fri.	7 50	Ar..Los Angeles..Lv.	8 25	Fri.	......	Sa.

a—Connection is bus operated. †Daily, except Sunday. c—Daily during Park season. d—Conditional Stop.

Timetable
circa 10-26-47

NORTH COAST
Limited

NORTHERN PACIFIC

YELLOWSTONE PARK LINE

*Main Street
of the
Northwest*

F 6111

Northern Pacific Train Number Schedule

The following train numbers are referred to in the photo captions. This list does not comprise all the NP trains.

Passenger and Mixed Trains

Number	Name	Between	Extra Information
1-2 (Till 11-15-52)	North Coast Limited	Chicago-Seattle	Passenger
25-26 (From 11-16-52)	North Coast Limited	Chicago-Seattle	Passenger
3-4 (Till 11-15-52)	Alaskan	St. Paul-Seattle	Passenger
1-2 (From 11-16-52)	Mainstreeter	St. Paul-Seattle	Passenger
5-6	(No Name)	Spokane-Seattle	Passenger
205-206	(No Name)	Billings-Red Lodge	Passenger
2nd Section NCL (WB)	Comet (1920's)	Chicago-Livingston	Passenger- Summer only.
2nd Section Alaskan (EB)	Comet (1920's)	Livingston-Chicago	
217-218	Comet (1920's)	Livingston-Gardiner	Passenger- June 10 to September
217-218	Park Train	Livingston-Gardiner	15 each year. Morning train.
221-222	Helena Stub	Logan-Helena	Passenger- NCL connection
233-234	Park Branch Local	Livingston-Gardiner	Passenger during tourist season, mixed during winter. Evening train.
235-236	Butte Stub	Logan-Butte	Passenger- Alaskan connection.
255-256	Coeur D' Alene Local	Missoula-Wallace	Passenger- In early years numbered 199-200 & 263-264.
311-312	Palouse	Spokane-Lewiston	Passenger
313-314	Palouse	Spokane-Lewiston	Passenger

Passenger and Mixed Trains

Number	Name	Between	Extra Information
315-316	Central Washington	Spokane-Coulee City	Passenger
407-408	Hot Shot	Portland-Seattle	Passenger
561-562	Local	Portland-Seattle	Passenger
(No Number)	Gyro Special	Wallace-Taft	Passenger- One time only on 7-18-58. A service organization celebration.

Freight Trains

Number	Name	Between	Extra Information
602-603	Time Freights and Tonnage Limited	Auburn-Northtown Northtown-Auburn	Freight- Important business
612	Overflow from No. 602	Auburn-Laurel Yard	Freight- Mostly CB&Q business.
651-652	Work Local	Livingston-Butte	Freight- Switch every possible situation. It was a clean-up job.
805-806	East Local	Branch lines out of Livingston and mainline Livingston-Laurel	Freight- Day of the week determined which job it worked.
(No Number)	Fruit Train	Pasco-Northtown	Freight- Mostly fruit.
(No Number)	"J" Manifest	Auburn-Northtown (Eastbound only)	Freight- All lumber train, mostly flat cars. Restricted to 35 mph due to shifting loads.

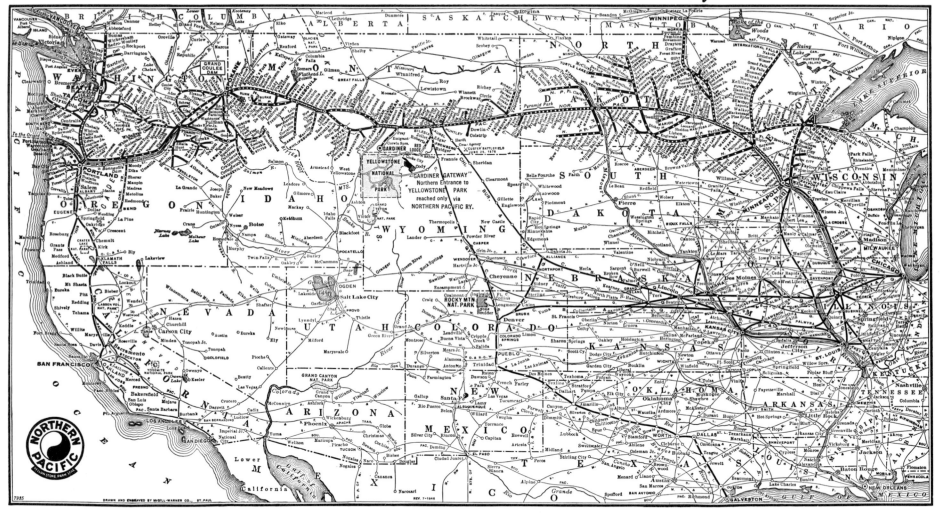

Northern Pacific system map from October, 1947 timetable.

General Motors No. 754 at Livingston, Montana on 11-3-46. This is one of the
few pictures of Warren and Ron together, usually one of them was shooting
the other. *"That's Road Foreman Charlie Simonsen just getting on the engine.
He was running it when the engine nearly derailed at Whitehall."* R.V. Nixon

Warren McGee

Warren McGee was born on September 7, 1914 to Howard and Mildred McGee. Warren was the second of five children born into a "train family". His father was an engineer with the NP for forty-three years from 1907 to 1950.

After graduating from Livingston, Montana's Park County High School in 1933, Warren found work as a "hand-shovel runner" for the National Park Service in Yellowstone Park. He also had some experience as a dishwasher, earning about one dollar a day. In 1936 at the age of 21, Warren began his career with the railroads as a brakeman for the Great Northern, working out of Seattle, Portland, Wenatchee, and Vancouver. World War II called him into the Air Force in 1942, during which time he served with a photo mapping and reconnaissance squadron. Warren was discharged a technical sergeant in September of 1945.

Upon returning to Montana, Warren began his thirty year association with the NP, signing on as a brakeman. After being promoted to conductor, he piloted trains from his home town of Livingston to Billings, Butte, and Helena until his retirement on the Freedom Train run through Montana in October of 1975.

Warren began taking railroad photographs in 1930 and now has a collection of over 30,000 negatives and slides (not all of railroad subjects however). He is frequently asked by various groups to give slide shows on railroads, river float trips, Bozeman Trail, and senior citizen trips. His railroad photos have appeared in every major railroad magazine and numerous books.

Mr. McGee has also been active in many local causes. He chaired the Livingston anti-merger committee and fought the Burlington Northern merger through the Supreme Court. In 1980, he and his wife Bernice were chosen Citizens of the Year for Livingston. He is presently the building superintendent for the Park County Museum in Livingston and is also a member of the city park board. Warren and Bernice were instrumental in rehabilitating a river course beside Livingston. Together they dug the holes and planted hundreds of trees along the river, which are now enjoyed by many fishermen.

Warren continues to reside in Livingston to this day. He says he is some two hundred letters behind in correspondence, but hopes to answer all of them someday, as soon as his trees and museum work lessens.

These two pictures document father and son's first passenger train run together. In the first photo, Conductor Warren McGee compares the time with his father, Engineer Harold McGee. Father and son combined for fifty-seven years of service to the NP. In the second photo, Warren hands train orders to his father in the cab of NP 6508 before departing from Livingston with Train No. 4 on 11-21-50. *W.R. McGee*

The crew of General Motors experimental train No. 754 after arriving at Butte, Montana on 11-3-46. Brakeman Warren McGee is on the far left. *R.V. Nixon*

Ron Nixon

Ron Nixon's grandparents came as pioneers to Montana by covered wagon before the Northern Pacific was completed. Ron was born on April 16, 1911 at Gardiner, Montana, the original entrance to Yellowstone Park.

Ron began taking pictures at the age of five. His first photos were of a circus that came to town, he still has the negatives. His mother, herself an excellent photographer, encouraged and helped educate him in the art. His first engine ride came when he was six, in the cab of No. 107, an NP 4-6-0. From then on Ron practically lived in the roundhouse. Also about this time, his father started him on a project of recording the engine number of each locomotive he saw, a practice he has carried on until this day. When he was nine, his mother taught him the dot-dash system of telegraphy.

After graduating from high school as class valedictorian, Ron went to work for the NP as a telegrapher at Livingston.

He hired out for a while in 1929 with the Canadian Pacific. From there he went to work for the NP's relay division, his "last job" with the NP. There were a few interruptions in this last job however; a year as a brewery accountant, a dispatcher for five years with the Great Northern, and a leave of absence at the Minneapolis Railroad School.

In 1939 the NP's advertising department became aware of Ron's talent and began using his photographs in their publications. Many have since appeared in the NP's calendars and publicity literature. Ron's collection of photographs is now in excess of 30,000, with about two-thirds of them railroad in nature. The collection includes pictures of nearly every locomotive the NP has ever owned, most of them taken by Ron himself. His photographs have appeared in every major railroad magazine and a large number of books.

Mr. Nixon was responsible for saving

NP 1356, a 4-6-0, and having it displayed by the station at Missoula. He helped engineer the rescue and restoration of NP 684, a 4-4-0 that was rusting away at Nez Perce, Idaho. Ron was also involved with the NP's most famous engine, No. 2626, the Timken Roller Bearing's "Four Aces", extensively photographing its final run on August 4, 1957. Ron and others were trying to work out a plan with Timken officials to put the locomotive on permanent display at Canton, Ohio, but the NP scrapped the engine before negotiations could be completed.

Ron is now retired and lives in Polson, Montana. Photography, railroad history, and fly fishing are just a few of his spare time activities. He would like to be remembered most for the enjoyment he is able to give others through his photographs.

Ron Nixon poses on the pilot of Northern Pacific No. 5000 at Glendive, Montana in September of 1932. *R.V. Nixon*

With his 4x5 Graphic, Ron captures Train No. 3 rounding the curve near Eddy, Montana, 7-2-52. *R.V. Nixon*

Chapter 2

Mikados 2-8-2

CLASS W

ALCO	2-8-2
Built:	1904-1907
160 Engines	1500-1659

Train No. 1 with NP 1585 arriving at Missoula, Montana nearly 24 hours late on 3-30-43. *"Class W engines were never assigned to the North Coast Limited. In this instance, the train was detoured over the Great Northern from Fargo and 1585 was the heaviest power they could use on some of the GN branches. The 1585 lost a lot of time on the GN and the No. 1 of the next day just about caught up with it at Missoula, the derailment having been cleared. Quite a rare coincidence, I have a picture of the same engine being used in emergency service out of Fargo on the No. 1 in 1938."* R.V. Nixon

Train No. 1 with 1539 and 2607 leading the way climbs Evaro Hill near Nagos, Montana, 9-20-39.
R.V. Nixon

Train No. 236 with NP 1525 on the point at a meeting with Train No. 1 (NP 1761 & 2605) at Spire Rock, Montana in June of 1933. Spire Rock is twenty miles east of Butte.
R.V. Nixon

Train No. 2 with 1536 & 2610 crossing Montana's Marent Trestle on 2-14-40. Prior to 1945 Marent Trestle couldn't carry any engine heavier than a Class A Northern and W-3 & W-5 Mikados.
R.V. Nixon

The Camas Prairie Extra with NP 1521 heading west between Reubens and Nucrag, Idaho on 5-24-51. Shot taken from a gondola. *"I took another picture toward the rear showing NP 684 being towed by this train."* R.V. Nixon

Camas Prairie Extra 1521 heading west near Lapwai, Idaho, 5-24-51. *R.V. Nixon*

Eastbound Extra 1548 photographed from the cab of NP 6513 on the double track mainline south of Tacoma, Washington on 6-18-51, both trains at speed. *"I think the 6513 was making close to 75 mph at the time."* R.V. Nixon

CLASS W-2

ALCO	2-8-2
Built:	1904-1905
20 Engines	1900-1919

Train No. 806, the East Local, with NP 1902 crossing the Boulder River at Big Timber, Montana on 10-16-40. The local will side dump a load of gravel in the cribs at the end of the bridge. This photo was Warren's first NP picture to appear in "Trains" magazine. *W.R. McGee*

Extra 1902 arriving on its regular Tuesday schedule at Wilsall, Montana on
11-28-39. *"It has 149 miles to travel today before getting back to Laurel. The
local will wait here at the end of the track while the crew is in the office getting
instructions from the agent on the loads and empties to be switched out.
Meanwhile, the engineer oils around and Brakeman McGee takes this picture."*
W.R. McGee

12

Second No. 1 with NP 2651, fifteen cars, and NP 1757 helping out, on its way up the 1.8% Bozeman Pass grade near Muir, Montana on 11-14-40. The North Coast Limited needed a helper on Bozeman Pass with anything over twelve cars. *W.R. McGee*

CLASS W-3

ALCO	2-8-2
Built:	1913-1920
125 Engines	1700-1834

NP 1802 in helper service for Train No. 562. Shown here at Tacoma, Washington on 4-12-39. *W.R. McGee*

14

Extra 1709 westbound with 3,146 tons (28 loads, 36 empties) at Greycliff,
Montana on 8-12-39. *W.R. McGee*

NP 1761 with twelve cars and Helper 1527, seen here one mile
east of Bozeman, Montana on 12-18-39. *W.R. McGee*

Eastbound No. 652 with NP 1809 and 2,582 tons of freight (45 loads, 39
empties) at the west end of Bozeman Tunnel on 7-25-40. The elevation here
is 5,592 feet. The sign in the picture commemorates Captain Clark's (of Lewis
and Clark) crossing of this pass in 1806. *W.R. McGee*

NP 1767 and the second section of Train No. 2 crossing Marent Trestle on 4-4-45. *"This is unusual and probably the only instance where W-3 freight engines were regularly assigned to the North Coast Limited. At the time, heavier power could not be used on the Flathead River Bridge east of Perma, Montana."* R.V. Nixon

Train No. 236 with NP 1761 makes its way up the 2.2% grade near Welch, Montana on 8-22-41. *W.R. McGee*

Extra 1710 heads west hauling 3,512 tons (35 loads, 23 empties). Bearcreek coal is at the head end with Rosebud coal behind that. The location is Reed Point, Montana in the one mile wide Yellowstone Valley. U.S. Highway 10 is at the bottom of this photo taken 11-1-40. *W.R. McGee*

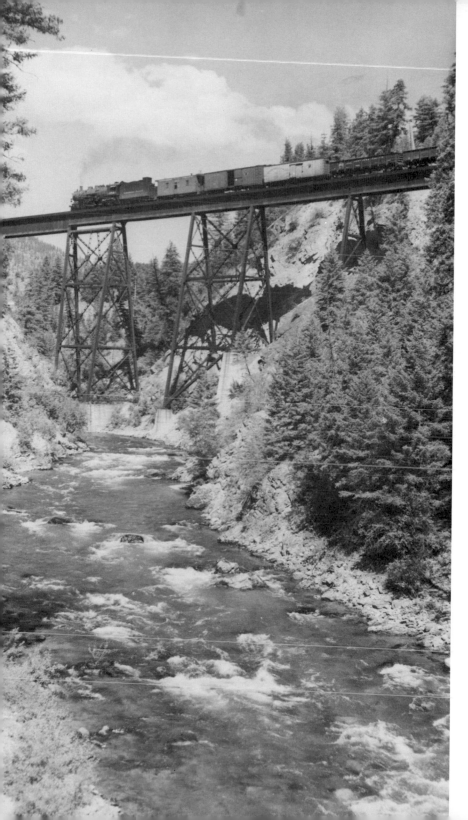

Extra 1722 East, the Atom Special, arriving at Pasco, Washington on 6-15-50. *R. V. Nixon*

Extra 1719 heads east over the Fish Creek trestle near Rivulet, Montana, 6-13-52. *R. V. Nixon*

Westbound Extra 1816-1770 leaving Spokane, Washington for Lewiston, Idaho on 9-5-50. *W.R. McGee*

Westbound Extra 1742 near Marshall, Washington on 4-13-51. *R.V. Nixon*

Eastbound Extra 1760, the Veteran's Special, leaving Polson, Montana on 6-14-53. This was the last passenger train to leave Polson. Flathead Lake is in the background. *R. V. Nixon*

Westbound Extra 1792 leaving Spokane, Washington on 8-3-53. *R. V. Nixon*

NP 2504 getting a load of coal at Mandan, North Dakota on 4-26-46. This engine was rebuilt in 1918 from a Class T 2-6-2 (No. 2322) and was scrapped at Brainerd on 12-4-58. *W.R. McGee*

CLASS W-4

ALCO	2-8-2
Built :	1906
6 Engines	2500-2505
Rebuilt from obsolete 2-6-2's	

Train No. 2, with NP 1845 & 2610, on the 2.2% grade west of Evaro, Montana on 10-5-39. *"Raining hard when I took this one."* R.V. Nixon

CLASS W-5

ALCO	2-8-2
Built:	1923
25 Engines	1835-1859

Train No. 602, with NP 1838 and 3,434 tons (66 loads, no empties), on the low line near DeSmet, Montana on 11-20-39. *W.R. McGee*

Eastbound Extra 1844 crossing the Clark Fork River at Huson, Montana on
12-4-39. The auxiliary tender in this photo is from a scrapped Class T 2-6-2.
The NP rebuilt a number of such tenders which were used mainly with W-5
class locomotives. It permited longer run assignments and also allowed them to
take on coal and water at the same time. This practice wasn't too common and
was outmoded as the larger, more modern locomotives arrived. *R.V. Nixon*

NP 1847, just out of the shops, at Livingston, Montana on 1-17-41. *W.R. McGee*

Extra 1854 East, the all lumber "J" Manifest, arriving at Rivulet, Montana on 6-8-43. *R.V. Nixon*

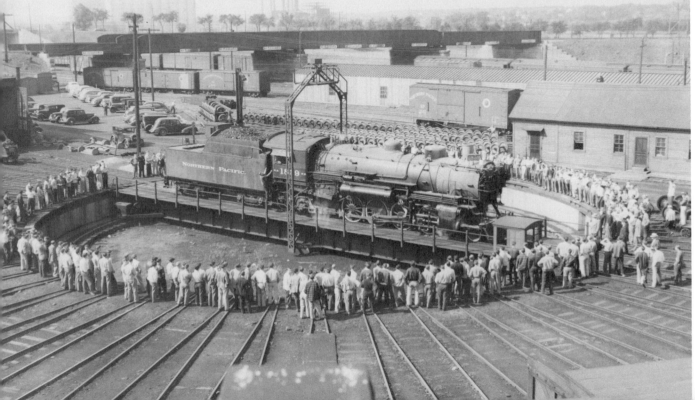

NP 1859 on the turntable at Northtown (Minneapolis), Minnesota on 6-23-48. *"This is the engine of the train I chartered for the students when I was with the Minneapolis Railroad School. The guys were very helpful in forming a circle around the engine for a picture. The next year on the GN at St. Cloud they weren't so cooperative."* R.V. Nixon

Train No. 255 with NP 2212 on Milwaukee Road tracks at Haugan, Montana on 4-18-41. *R. V. Nixon*

CLASS Q-4

49 Engines	4-6-2
2177-2207	Baldwin 1909-10
2208-2225	ALCO 1910

NP 2210 and Train No. 314's three cars at Lewiston, Idaho on 2-18-41.
W.R. McGee

Train No. 255 with NP 2212 at Cyr, Montana on 4-18-41. This was the last run of the Missoula-Wallace passenger train after nearly fifty years of continuous service. *R.V. Nixon*

Continuing its last run, Train No. 255 waits on the siding for the Milwaukee Road's No. 16 at St. Regis, Montana. *R.V. Nixon*

A final shot of Train No. 255 as it passes into history. The location is Borax, Montana on 4-18-41. *R.V. Nixon*

Train No. 221 with NP 2213 at Trident, Montana on 5-30-41. After this photo was taken, the steel pilot was replaced with a wooden one. *"This is the only instance I've known of where a wooden pilot replaced one of steel." R.V. Nixon*

Train No. 315 at Spokane, Washington on 7-28-51. This was one of the 2222's last runs. *"The NP sure ruined its appearance in later years compared to the way it looked most of the time with its traditional wooden pilot and without numberboards."* R.V. Nixon

Train No. 3 at Bismarck, North Dakota on 1-22-40. The square bulge on the side of 2244's smokebox was due to the Coffin feedwater heater inside. *W.R. McGee*

CLASS Q-5	
ALCO	4-6-2
Built:	1920
20 Engines	2226-2245

NP 2239, just out of the shops following a class one overhaul, at Livingston, Montana on 3-28-39. *W.R. McGee*

Locomotive 2245 with Train No. 4's eight cars begins its climb of the 1.9% Bozeman Pass grade on 11-14-39. Superintendant's Car No. 1900 is along for the ride. *W.R. McGee*

NP 2245 and Train No. 4 on the 1.9% mountain grade at Rocky Canyon, Montana on 11-14-39. *W.R. McGee*

Train No. 3 with NP 2239 waits on the siding for Train No. 2 at Perma, Montana on 5-20-44. This is the engine that overturned near Athol on 6-13-41. The crew on a Spokane International freight estimated the speed at 100 miles per hour. *R.V. Nixon*

Train No. 4, with NP 2235 and Helper 1522, near Montellis, Montana on 7-29-40. *R.V. Nixon*

NP 2232 and the nine car Train No. 4 near the headwaters of the Missouri
River at Clarkston, Montana on 6-6-41. *R.V. Nixon*

NP 2238 with help from NP 1808 takes the nine car North Coast Limited up the 2.2% grade at Welch, Montana on 8-22-41. Note the other two trains in the background on both sides of 2238's smokestack. *W.R. McGee*

Train No. 4 with NP 2236 and 2231 leaving Glendive, Montana on 3-10-44.
R.V. Nixon

Train No. 2 with NP 2239 crosses
Montana's Marent Trestle on
4-4-45. *R.V. Nixon*

Steam power on the North Coast
Limited was as follows:
Until 1926: Class Q   4-6-2's
1926-1934: Class A   4-8-4's
1934-1938: Class A-2 4-8-4's
1938-1941: Class A-3 4-8-4's
1941-1947: Class A-4 4-8-4's

NP 2245 helping Train No. 2 out of Arlee, Montana on 7-30-41. "*Steamers were prohibited from pushing on the swanky observation cars, but I caught them doing it a couple of times.*" The observation car is on loan from the Pennsylvania Railroad and was used by the NP while theirs was in the shops. Although this was a fairly common practice, this is the only picture I have ever seen of another railroad's observation car on an NP train. *R.V. Nixon*

Two views of Train No. 1, with NP 2240, 2235, and 1858, leaving Livingston on 9-21-47. This train has some of the new lightweight passenger cars. The first of these built were Coaches 500-517 (in 1946). Diners were next in 1947, with the rest arriving between 1947 and 1948 (observation cars being the last in 1948). This equipment was not put into regular service on the NP until November of 1952. *W.R. McGee*

Above: Train No. 4 with NP 2247 taking on water and getting the once over before leaving Yakima, Washington on 9-26-45. *W.R. McGee*

At left: Train No. 4, the Alaskan, with NP 2245 on a cold, cold day near Trident, Montana on 1-3-47. *W.R. McGee*

CLASS Q-6	
ALCO	4-6-2
Built:	1923
20 Engines	2246-2265

49

Above: Train No. 4 with NP 2263 leaving Seattle, Washington on 8-30-48. The clock tower of Seattle's King Street Station can be seen in the background. *R. V. Nixon*

At left: NP 2251 at the Paradise, Montana coal dock prior to pulling out with Train No. 4 in March of 1930. *R. V. Nixon*

Train No. 4 with seven cars in tow pulls into the station at Pasco, Washington on 5-17-39. *W.R. McGee*

Above: Train No. 2 with NP 2246 and 2256 passes the derailed NP 5107 west of Trout Creek, Montana on 9-7-44. Two years earlier the 5107 derailed in almost the same position at Turah, Montana. Trout Creek was the halfway point of the 186 mile trip from Paradise, Montana to Spokane, Washington. *"I think at one time or another the 2256 handled every scheduled passenger run on the NP." R.V. Nixon*

At left: Train No. 5 with NP 2259 and five cars along the Yakima River, one mile east of Wymer, Washington on 5-5-41. *W.R. McGee*

Westbound Extra 2260 at Spokane, Washington on 5-2-53. *R. V. Nixon*

CLASS A

ALCO	4-8-4
Built:	1926-1927
12 Engines	2600-2611

In her gray boiler jacket, Locomotive 2601 waits at Livingston, Montana on 11-29-41. This engine was built by ALCO in November of 1926 and was scrapped 33 years later at South Tacoma on 11-26-59. *W.R. McGee*

NP 2607 at Logan, Montana in May of 1930. *"2607 was one of NP's best. 2603 was the lemon of this class. I purposely got the old guy in the picture as he was a fixture around Logan. He met every train to carry mail to the post office."* R.V. Nixon

Inside the Livingston shops in May of 1933. Locomotive 2611 is in the foreground. This was the NP's largest shop and the only one that could accommodate the 5000 and 5100 series locomotives.
R.V. Nixon

Train No. 1 with NP 2600 at Whitehall, Montana in June of 1932. This photo was taken from the top of the coal dock.
R.V. Nixon

NP 2610 at Missoula, Montana, 8-8-38. *W.R. McGee*

NP 2607 at Livingston, Montana on New Years Day 1940. *W. R. McGee*

Train No. 1 with NP 2610 leaving Missoula, Montana on 3-6-40. Alongside is General Motors 103, the first diesel to pull the North Coast Limited. The coal dock in the background was later torn down and replaced with a new one. *"This would appear to be a case of poor judgement, what with diesels already on the scene."* R.V. Nixon

Two views of Train No. 2 with NP 2611 racing the Milwaukee Road Olympian near Nimrod, Montana on 4-14-41. *R.V. Nixon*

NP 2601, just out of the shops, at Livingston on 11-29-41. *W.R. McGee*

Train No. 3 with NP 2604
between Eddy and Woodlin,
Montana on 6-11-44. *R.V. Nixon*

Train No. 3, with NP 2604 and
Helper 1714, seen here three and
one-half miles west of Livingston
on 2-8-47. *W.R. McGee*

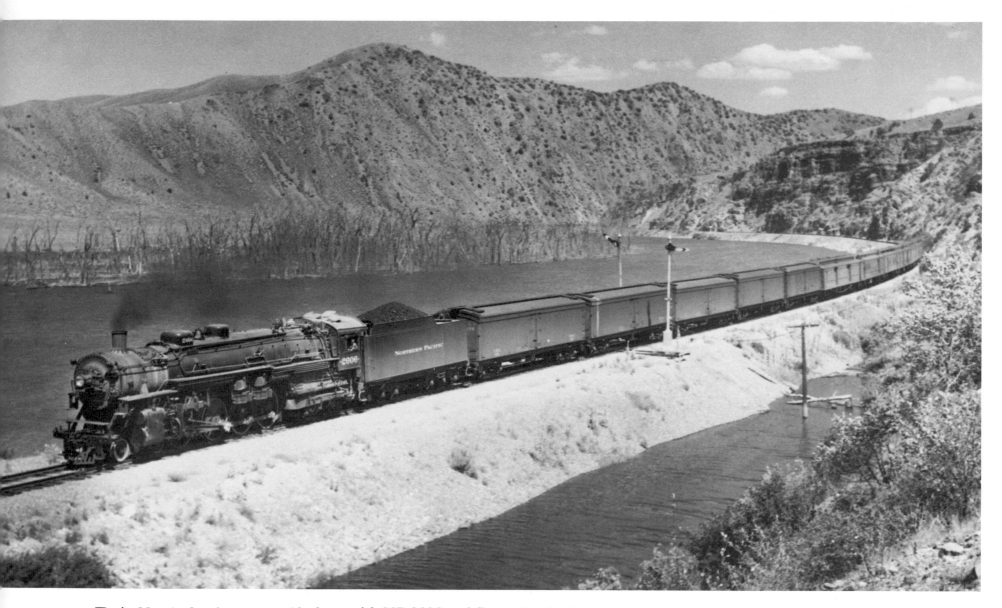

Train No. 4, the sixteen car Alaskan, with NP 2606 and five carloads of cherries, along the Missouri River on 7-28-47. This photo was taken in the area dammed by Toston Dam near Lombard, Montana. Express reefers were not always used on the Alaskan or North Coast Limited, usually only when they had fragile fruit, excess express, or when salmon was in season. *W.R. McGee*

NP 2606 and the twelve car Train No. 3 climbs the 2.2% grade over Montana's Skyline Trestle with help from NP 1843 on 5-30-48. *W.R. McGee*

Train No. 1 with Timken 1111, the "Four Aces", at Logan, Montana in January of 1932. This locomotive had a profound influence not only on the NP, but on all mainline railroads. For many years the Timken Roller Bearing Company had been conducting tests advocating the use of roller bearings on steam locomotives, but failed to convince any railroad to put them into use. Timken even offered to do the installation free of charge, but still could find no takers. Finally they had ALCO construct a special roller bearing equipped locomotive expressly for demonstration purposes. In April of 1930 the Timken engine began test runs over several major railroads, finally arriving on the NP late in 1931. The locomotive's performance proved quite impressive. The roller bearings produced only one-twentieth of the starting friction of normal bearings. On 2-8-33 the NP purchased the Timken engine for about $33,000 and renumbered it 2626. *R.V. Nixon*

CLASS A-1

ALCO	4-8-4
Built:	1930
1 Engine	2626

Train No. 1 with Timken 1111 passing through Willow Creek, Montana in December of 1932. *"I have three favorite engines: Timken 1111 (later NP 2626), NP 684, and NP 1356. I was successful in saving 684 and 1356, but after a lot of hard work on the 2626, they scrapped it before negotiations could be finished. Too bad, as it was probably the most historic modern steamer, having worked on fifteen railroads and the fact that it was the first roller bearing engine. The speed record for the 1111 on its trial trips was set at the spot where this picture was taken, 88 miles per hour according to the tape in the dynamometer car. That's my dad standing at the west end of the depot."* R.V. Nixon

Timken 1111 on its first trip west at Livingston on 12-22-31. A very cold day with temperatures way below zero. An official rode in the box by the cylinders to check on the valve gear, etc. It must have been very uncomfortable on a day as cold as this. This engine was painted dark green with gold stripping during trial runs and when first acquired by the NP. *R.V. Nixon*

NP 2626 and a troop train running as the Second No. 3 departs from Missoula, Montana on 7-30-44. *R.V. Nixon*

NP 2626 on the turntable at Parkwater (Spokane), Washington on 4-18-40.
Both engine and tender were extensively rebuilt shortly after this picture
was taken. *W.R. McGee*

NP Timken 2626 at Lester, Washington, 8-4-57. *R. V. Nixon*

Train No. 1, NP 2651 and 2650 with eleven cars, leaves Livingston seven hours late on 11-13-40 because of a cold wave in Minnesota. *W.R. McGee*

<hr>

CLASS A-2

<hr>

Baldwin	4-8-4
Built:	1934-1935
10 Engines	2650-2659

Train No. 4 with NP 2652 and six cars at Helena, Montana on 2-26-38. *W.R. McGee*

72

Train No. 1 with NP 2651 at Logan, Montana, 1-22-39. *W.R. McGee*

Train No. 1 with NP 2651 and ten cars at Butte, Montana on 1-29-39.
Butte was always the preference for passenger runs because they had a
Union Pacific connection and quite spectacular scenery along the way.
*"As a conductor, I would tell the passengers coming out of Billings that
they would have the prettiest train ride in the United States between
Billings and Butte."* Santa Claus trains ran to Butte because of the
amount of mail in the area. *"I suppose by direction of the Post Office."*
When something would happen on the Helena line, they would have
to reroute all the freight trains through Butte. None of the sidings
on the Butte line held over seventy freight cars, so it was quite a job
of railroading to run them over this route. *W.R. McGee*

Train No. 1 with NP 2651 and 2650 leaves Livingston on 5-25-39. Just out of the shops, 2651 is on the point for this break-in trip. *W.R. McGee*

Second No. 1 with NP 2653 and eight cars at Welch, Montana on Butte
Mountain's 2.2% grade, 8-16-39. *W.R. McGee*

Train No. 1 with NP 2650 and eleven cars at Garrison, Montana on
11-17-39. *W.R. McGee*

Extra 2652 West at Paradise, Montana on 2-12-40. *"This was the first engine heavier than a Class A to arrive in Paradise. A special train with the 2652 and one car, Business Car 1900, was run from Missoula to Spokane on this date to make tests, particularly to check clearances."* R.V. Nixon

78

Second No. 603 with NP 2656 at Northtown (Minneapolis), Minnesota on 5-18-40. Beginning its hot-shot run for Seattle hauling 2,991 tons (with a 3,000 ton limit), it's due there in fifty-nine hours. *W.R. McGee*

NP 2650 with a troop train running west of Livingston as the second section of Train No. 1 on 8-4-40. *R.V. Nixon*

Train No. 1, NP 2651 with twelve cars and Helper 1761, on the 2.2% grade near Welch, Montana on 9-22-40. *W.R. McGee*

NP 2651 with the Second No. 1, a fifteen car Navy Recruit Special, descending Bozeman Pass near West End, Montana on 11-14-40. *W.R. McGee*

Second No. 1 with NP 2650 and seven cars at Big Spring (Rocky Canyon), Montana on 7-30-41. The North Coast Limited was usually run in two sections during the summer and holiday seasons. We'll follow this train over the next two pages. *W.R. McGee*

Now a little farther down the line, NP 2650 and the No. 1 are photographed near Chestnut, Montana. This engine was showcased at the Chicago Worlds Fair in September of 1934. It had been rushed from the Baldwin plant to appear in the "Wings of Progress" show as the grand finale. *"It was quite a sight. The 2650 was stopped in the middle of the stage after all the other engines, including practically every historic engine, had previously crossed it."* R.V. Nixon

Now five miles east of Butte, the No. 1 begins its descent of the 2.2% grade near Skones, Montana.
W.R. McGee

84

Eastbound Extra 2656 at Billings, Montana on 8-1-49. The A-2's were
assigned to freight service after the diesels came. *R.V. Nixon*

CLASS A-3

Baldwin	4-8-4
Built:	1938
8 Engines	2660-2667

NP 2661 at St. Paul, Minnesota on 5-17-40. In the days before number boards, the engine number went on the sand dome. *"What a clean, shiny engine. Not the way they looked during the last days of steam."* W.R. McGee

NP 2662 and Class Q-5 2230, the outgoing power for the two sections of Train No. 4, in front of the station at Livingston on 3-21-39. This station was built between 1901 and 1902, the original depot having been built about 1890. Note the NP logo made from river rock on the station lawn just over the 2230's cab. *"It was a beautiful piece of work with its raised curved portion, but was later destroyed as a liability to the cost conscious railroad management."* The track on the lower left is the Yellowstone Park Branch. *W.R. McGee*

NP 2665 and the eleven car North Coast Limited leaving Jamestown,
North Dakota on 1-20-40. *W.R. McGee*

While Extra 1766 waits on the siding, NP 2667 and the eleven car North Coast Limited passes through Quebec, Montana on 7-27-40. *W.R. McGee*

First No. 2 with NP 2664, and Second No. 2 with NP 2666, at Livingston on 8-8-41. These two trains were held at Livingston all night because of a washout sixty miles away at Craver, Montana. The old yard office on the right was Livingston's first depot. *W.R. McGee*

NP 2665 with Train No. 1 leaving Whitehall, Montana on 10-12-41. This was the first A-3 to work west of Livingston. *R.V. Nixon*

NP 2666, just out of the shops on a break-in trip, being used in helper service on Train No. 1 west of Livingston, 9-23-43. *R.V. Nixon*

Two views of NP 2662 and Train No. 1 as photographed on 2-8-47. At left, the train makes its way up the 1.8% grade eight miles west of Livingston at Hoppers Tunnel, Montana. At right, we catch up with it again on Bozeman Pass as it is just about to enter Bozeman Tunnel at Muir, Montana.
W.R. McGee

NP 2661 on the turntable at Livingston on 6-27-53. This engine was built by Baldwin in April of 1938 and was scrapped a little over twenty years later at Brainerd, Minnesota in May of 1958. *W.R. McGee*

Westbound 2670 at Laurel Yard, Montana on 10-6-41. The first run of an A-4, pulling a train consisting of only the superintendent's private car. *"It looked strange compared to the eighteen and twenty car trains we were accustomed to. Sort of a test trip to measure clearances."* New from Baldwin on 9-12-41, it soon began regular service on Train's No. 1 and 2 between St. Paul and Livingston, until relieved by diesel power in February of 1947. *W.R. McGee*

CLASS A-4

Baldwin	4-8-4
Built:	1941
8 Engines	2670-2677

NP 2670 cutting off Train No. 1 at Livingston on 10-13-41. This engine will make the 904 mile return trip to St. Paul on the No. 2 at ten o'clock tonight. *"The A-4's were the ultimate steam power on the NP. They were built in the 1940's with an all steel pilot that was later prohibited on the A-5's due to tight regulations on the use of excess steel during the war. This pilot was suppose to throw an automobile completely off the right-of-way when they hit one."* The large tender on this engine held twenty-seven tons of coal and twenty-five thousand gallons of water. *W.R. McGee*

Brand new NP 2676 making her first trip into Livingston from St. Paul on 11-8-41. *W.R. McGee*

Train No. 2 with NP 2673 and eleven cars, leaving Jamestown, North Dakota on 4-26-46. *W.R. McGee*

Here's how the 2673 looked three years later on 5-25-49 at Glendive, Montana on the head end of Train No. 4. Note the new numberboards on the side of the smokebox. *W.R. McGee*

Second No. 1 with NP 2675 leaving St. Paul, Minnesota on 7-5-48. *"This is one of my favorite shots. For several years I worked on the eleventh floor of one of the buildings in the background and could see all St. Paul passenger train movements from the window."* R.V. Nixon

Second No. 1 on the stone arch bridge at Minneapolis, Minnesota on 8-23-48. *"This was one of the most hazardous shots I ever made. I was perched five stories up on the slanting roof of a power plant."* R.V. Nixon

Westbound Extra 2674, an eleven car Army Special, along the Gallatin River at Logan, Montana on 1-3-51. The A-4's seldom went west of Livingston. *W.R. McGee*

NP 2676, in its beautiful gray color scheme, glides onto the turntable at Livingston on 6-27-53. Some of the engines from each of the different Northern classes, and the Q-5 and Q-6 Pacifics, had their boilers painted gray. The shade was a little darker than the light gray used on the Union Pacific's two-tone gray scheme. The NP used this scheme from the late 1930's through the end of steam, with some engines being scrapped in gray. But just because an engine was painted gray, didn't mean that it would stay that way. Later it might be painted black, as there was no set pattern. *W.R. McGee*

CLASS A-5

Baldwin	4-8-4
Built:	1943
10 Engines	2680-2689

Extra 2681, on its way east with a load of fruit, is photographed near Irvin, Washington on 2-22-53. *"Howard Fogg made a splendid painting from this photo which was later reproduced on a Christmas card."* R.V. Nixon

NP 2685, 2663, and 2687, each on a different section of Train No. 1, at
Livingston on 2-15-46. *R. V. Nixon*

NP 2680 lays on her side at Flynn, Montana on 4-23-46 while the crew decides what to do next. Earlier in the day Train No. 224, an equipment special, had a car go on the ties and tore the rail from the spikes going into the siding. The signal bonds on the track had not been broken however, so the 2680 and her westbound train of twenty-six troop cars didn't find out about it until it was too late. Five cars were damaged, but luckily no one was hurt. *W.R. McGee*

"You couldn't tell by looking, but this was the second section of the North Coast Limited at Dilworth, Minnesota on 8-10-50. The 2681 dwarfs the stream-lined coaches." At Manitoba Junction the Winnipeg cars were picked up which made it a full size train by the time it rolled into the Twin Cities. *R.V. Nixon*

Two views of NP 2687 and the Second No. 1, a fifteen car Korean War Army Special, on 5-4-52. Helper 1808 brings up the rear. In the top photo, the train is just leaving Livingston. In the lower photo, we catch up with it again working the 1.8% grade approximately three miles further west.
W.R. McGee

NP 2686 at Livingston on 8-15-52. The A-5 class locomotives were built during
World War II at a time when the use of excess steel was prohibited due to
government regulations. Lightweight silicon steel was unavailable, so heavier
carbon steel was used for boiler construction. Cast steel bells were used rather
than brass ones. The A-5 was the second heaviest 4-8-4, outweighed only
by the Santa Fe's 2900 class locomotives. *W.R. McGee*

Second No. 2 with NP 2681 at
Spokane, Washington on 10-12-52.
R. V. Nixon

Eastbound Extra 2689 leaving
Paradise, Montana on 8-15-54.
R. V. Nixon

Train No. 4 with NP 2681 at Glendive, Montana on 6-14-56. This was the last passenger run assigned to steam, and the only reason steam was used was because it eliminated a diesel layover for a day at Glendive. Diesels were used on the St. Paul to Mandan No. 3 and then returned immediately on the No. 4. *"I made a special trip to Glendive to get pictures of the last steam run and rode the 2681 to Mandan. It was quite a memorable trip. Too bad the NP didn't keep the steamers clean after the diesels came."* R.V. Nixon

CLASS Z

Baldwin	2-6-6-2
Built:	1907
16 Engines	3000-3015

NP 3014 at Wallace, Idaho on 2-14-38. The NP ran these on a trial basis out of Livingston in 1904. Although intended for road service, they spent most of their lives working as helpers. They were exactly the same as the Great Northern's 1800 series engines. *W.R. McGee*

CLASS Z-1

Baldwin	2-6-6-2
Built:	1910
6 Engines	3100-3105

NP 3100 at Wallace, Idaho on 5-20-38. In search of a better road engine, the NP had six of these, but they never turned out to be much of a success. As train lengths and tonnage increased, heavier and more powerful engines were needed. The Z-1's were very slow, and attempting any speed over ten miles per hour with their fifty-five inch drivers resulted in great abuse to the engine and track. They served out most of their time with the NP on the Wallace Branch. The 3100 ended up with the Rayonier Logging Company near Hoquiam, Washington. *W.R. McGee*

NP 4025 crosses U.S. Highway 10 just below Borax, Montana on 7-31-51.
R.V. Nixon

CLASS Z-3

21 Engines	2-8-8-2
ALCO 1913	4005-4014
ALCO 1917	4015-4019
ALCO 1920	4020-4025

Train No. 255 with NP 2212 at a meeting with eastbound Extra 4021 on Milwaukee Road tracks at Haugan, Montana on 4-18-41. This was the last run for No. 255 (See pages 33-36). *R.V. Nixon*

Second No. 603 with NP 4017 and 2,950 tons of freight train along the Yakima
River at Umtanum, Washington, 5-5-41. *W.R. McGee*

Two more views of Train No. 603 as it winds its way along the Yakima River on 5-5-41. At left, near Teanaway, Washington. Above, at Nelson, Washington. *W.R. McGee*

Westbound Extra 4025 on the NP-Milwaukee Road interchange along the Clark Fork River at St. Regis, Montana on 4-14-43. *R. V. Nixon*

Eastbound NP 4025 along the
St. Regis River near the old town
of Taft, Montana on 4-15-43.
R.V. Nixon

Westbound NP 4021 crosses U.S.
Highway 10 near Borax, Montana
on 9-28-45. *R.V. Nixon*

Westbound Extra 5132, with Helper's 4008 and 4012, hauls forty-seven carloads of coal weighing upwards of 4,500 tons up the 1.8% grade at Hoppers Tunnel, Montana on 5-29-46. This tunnel was daylighted in 1952. *"These were non-revenue trains, nothing but company coal from Colstrip, Montana. We would handle one of these every three or four days. Unit coal trains are not a new idea."* W.R. McGee

120

In the top photo, westbound NP 4025 meets with the Milwaukee Road's Class E-12 No. 18 at Henderson, Montana. *"Sadly, trains of both roads are now discontinued and the track has been removed."* In the lower view, the 4025 is photographed at the top of Lookout Pass. The track descends at a steady 4% grade in either direction from this point. *"Big train! That's my brother standing by the caboose."* R.V. Nixon

Westbound Extra 4025 climbs the 4% grade approaching Lookout Pass, Montana on 7-31-51. *"This line was probably the most spectacular and historic of any on the NP."* U.S. Highway 10 is visible on the left. *R.V. Nixon*

NP 4025 along the St. Regis River near Saltese, Montana on 4-18-52. This is on the Wallace Branch, between Wallace and Missoula. The tracks on the other side of the river belong to the Milwaukee Road. *W.R. McGee*

NP 4025 at Arlee, Montana on 1-9-58. *"This is a sad one. The 4025 was the last of the compound mallets and was being hauled dead to South Tacoma for scrapping. It resisted however, by running hot and had to be set out at Arlee for further movement the next day. The diesel was on Train No. 2, which added insult to injury." R.V. Nixon*

CLASS Z-4

ALCO	2-8-8-2
Built:	1923
4 Engines	4500-4503

Helpers 4500 and 1781 pushing 4,400 tons of coal west of Livingston on 1-29-41. *"I'd think the crew in the flimsy caboose would have been a trifle nervous."* This USRA type hardly ever worked west of Garrison, Montana. They saw most of their service on the Rocky Mountain Division. When the Z-5 5000's got over to the Helena area, the Z-4's were bumped out. The Z-4's were scrapped in the early 1950's. *R.V. Nixon*

124

CLASS Z-5

12 Engines	2-8-8-4
ALCO 1929	5000
Baldwin 1930	5001-5011

NP 5006 at Livingston on 6-10-41, after being re-built with roller bearings and a new frame. *"They stopped all conversation in Livingston when they left town on the end of a train. The noise pounded your ear drums and their immensity was quite a sight to behold."* R.V. Nixon

Above: Westbound Extra 5010 as photographed from the cab of the NP's first road diesel, No. 6000, at Sentinel Butte, North Dakota on 3-10-44. *R.V. Nixon*

At left: Eastbound Extra 5003 departs Glendive, Montana in March of 1939. *R.V. Nixon*

NP 5008 at Wataga, Montana on a break-in trip fresh from the Livingston shops on 6-11-38. This was the first Z-5 to have a doghouse installed on its tender, reducing its water capacity by fifty gallons. The fat balloon smokestack was replaced with a standard size one in 1941. The Z-5's worked as far west as Garrison, Montana. Two of these locomotives were assigned to helper service on the high line out of Helena. *W.R. McGee*

NP 5003 on the turntable at Livingston on 5-21-41 after being rebuilt with a new frame and roller bearings. *"The Z-5's, although somewhat slow, saved the NP millions by being able to haul a full tonnage train between Glendive and Mandan, where in the past, trains had to be cut in half. The Z-5's were improved considerably in 1941 when the NP rebuilt them. And powerful! I've heard engineers say a Z-5 would pull anything the drawbars would hold. The NP had very few fizzles. Probably the Class P-3 4-6-0's (1400-1419) were the worst, and the Class T 2-6-2's (2300-2449) were top-heavy and not very powerful."* R.V. Nixon

NP 5000 helps out the first train to enter the new Bozeman Tunnel on 7-28-45. During most of their careers the Z-5's were restricted to thirty-five miles per hour. In the late 1940's they bought new frames for them and had the cylinders cast integral. They also added roller bearings and bricked up the front grate section to make them steam better. After that they could run them up to fifty miles per hour. The 5000 had a short stubby smokestack on her when first built, but it lasted only two months before being replaced. *"They sure could chew up the coal and water."* R.V. Nixon

129

NP 5000 helping a westbound diesel extra west of Livingston on 6-27-50.
This was the 5000's last assignment after having put in nearly twenty years
of hauling trains across the badlands between Glendive and Mandan.
R.V. Nixon

Train No. 602 with NP 5011 and 4,283 tons, two miles west of Sully Springs in the North Dakota Badlands on 4-25-46. This area is now a large expanse of oil fields. *"The Z-5's were built especially for service in the bad-water district between Glendive and Mandan, where we had been double-heading the Mikados. The NP wanted to eliminate double-heading and still get 4,000 tons across the line and the Z-5's were one of the efforts they went through to see that it happened. Then, when they went to diesels, tonnage was reduced to 3,000 tons in order to maintain schedules."* W.R. McGee

Chapter 7
Challengers
4-6-6-4

CLASS Z-6	
21 Engines	4-6-6-4
5100-5111	ALCO 1936
5112-5120	ALCO 1937

Westbound Extra 5115 departs from Spokane, Washington with 3,010 tons on 9-6-50. *"The 5100 ran to Logan on its first break-in trip. Logan was forty-nine miles west of Livingston over the mountains and back. The master mechanic and everyone else who could get in the cab went along. West of Bozeman there was a twenty-four mile stretch of straight track and they wanted to let her out and see what she would do. They ran sixty to eighty miles per hour and had a hot driver box by the time they got to Logan. We had it on the drop pit in Logan trying to repack the hot box. The master mechanic said: 'Oil in here a little bit Walt.' Walt stuck his oil can in there and oiled the master mechanic."* W.R. McGee

Brand new class Z-6 engines 5113, 5114, and 5115 at Parkwater (Spokane), Washington in May of 1937. *R. V. Nixon*

Eastbound Extra 5105 met with disaster at West End, Montana in October of 1937. This was the hard luck engine on the NP. Besides this wreck, the boiler blew up at Willis. This engine was the first Z-6 to be scrapped at Brainerd on 10-19-54. *R. V. Nixon*

NP 5105 coming out of the shops at Livingston on 11-10-39 after an extensive overhaul. *"This was after the boiler explosion which killed five people at Willis, Montana (twenty-seven miles east of Missoula) on 7-7-38. The engineer was noted for running low water. During the rebuild they made several changes to this locomotive to make sure it wouldn't happen again. It was out of service for seven months and ten days, and was very nearly scrapped. ALCO bid $51,000 to rebuild her, but the NP shops did the job for $47,602.60."*
W.R. McGee

Eastbound Extra 5107 with 3,600 tons on the west slope of Bozeman Pass at Chestnut, Montana on 7-18-38. *W.R. McGee*

This shot was taken from the water tank at Pasco, Washington on 5-17-39.
Locomotives 5119, 5120, 5117, 1276, and 1269 are in view. Pasco was where
most of the tonnage originated. After a train would arive in Pasco (with a lot
of fruit from the Yakima Valley) they would try to build a train that was 4,000
tons to send over the line to Minneapolis. *W.R. McGee*

NP 5100 and the second section of Train No. 602 with Helper 4500 and 3,810 tons (70 loads/2 empties) at Bozeman, Montana on 6-10-39. *"The NP went to great lengths during the 1910-1940 era to haul a 4,000 ton train eastbound with just one locomotive. One of these efforts was the construction in 1919 of the water-grade Low Line between Bozeman and Logan. Although nine miles longer than the mainline (or High Line), it possessed an easier grade and was normally used only by eastbound freight trains. Westbound freights and all passenger trains used the shorter High Line. The eastbound freight in this picture is coming off the Low Line, with the helper (smoke on the horizon) showing the direction of the track. Installation of CTC between Helena and Livingston, as well as the new, more powerful diesels, eliminated use of the Low Line and it was removed in 1957."* W.R. McGee

Train No. 602 with NP 5103 eastbound on the 1% grade at Placer, Montana on 6-24-39. *W.R. McGee*

Train No. 602, with NP 5107 and 4501 helping out, rolls eastward with 3,991 tons over Bozeman Pass and is photographed at Rocky Canyon Milepost 133 on 7-2-39. *"Although it was only a 1.9% grade, this was the toughest pull on the whole railroad because of the reverse curves. A train would get all the way from Seattle and then stall here. If a break-in-two was going to occur, this is where it would happen."* W.R. McGee

Extra 5100 with 125 cars passing the section house at Chestnut, Montana on its way down the west side of Bozeman Pass on 11-20-39. *"Our men were good firemen, you very seldom saw much smoke. Rosebud coal burned so clean you could hardly see it anyway. Another reason I didn't get much smoke in my photos was because engineers thought any photographer was an official, and they would get reprimanded for a lot of smoke. Sometimes they would speed up their engines to try and make the photo blur. I would compensate for this by simply increasing my shutter speed."* W.R. McGee

Locomotive 5105 on Livingston's 135 foot long turntable, 11-22-39. *"Those fellows in the cab were wondering what the hell was wrong with me. In those days, if you took your camera in the roundhouse, you would stop all activity. Naturally, that made the roundhouse foreman declare open season on all photographers."* W.R. McGee

Just out of Bozeman Tunnel,
eastbound Train No. 602 with
NP 5105 and 3,688 tons is photographed at Muir, Montana on
12-4-39. This train broke in two
in the middle of the tunnel.
"Jinx engine 5105 strikes again!"
W.R. McGee

Extra 5106 eastbound near Townsend Hill, Montana on 12-12-39. This stretch between Townsend and Winston (15.3 miles) is one of the longest between sidings on any railroad. A thirty minute delay in meeting superior trains was not unusual. *W.R. McGee*

Westbound Extra 5111, stalled with 4,664 tons, at Livingston on Christmas Day 1939. *"Very cold!"* W.R. McGee

Westbound Extra 5104, with 3,196 tons and NP 4500 helping out, on the 1.8% grade four miles out of Livingston on 1-1-40. *"This was the way the NP usually moved coal. Almost every freight train in steam days (except No. 603) had fifteen to twenty cars of Rosebud coal on it for tonnage."* W.R. McGee

Third Train No. 1, a Civilian Conservation Corps Special, with NP 5106 and twelve cars, working the 1.8% grade some seven miles west of Livingston on 1-10-40. *W.R. McGee*

A little farther along, Train No. 1 is now photographed passing through
Chestnut, Montana. *W.R. McGee*

Extra 5120 westbound near Grass
Valley, Montana on 10-31-43.
This piece of track has since been
eliminated by a line change.
R. V. Nixon

Eastbound Extra 5107 leaving
Bozeman Tunnel at Muir, Montana
on 1-10-40. On its way down the
1.8% grade to Livingston, some
twelve miles away. This is the
highest point on the railroad with
an elevation of 5,592 feet.
W.R. McGee

Extra 5109 westbound with 3,455 tons at Lombard, Montana on 10-7-40.
We've just crossed Sixteen Mile Creek Bridge at the point where it meets the
Missouri River, after having picked up some cars at the Milwaukee Road
interchange. *"A lot of this hillside came down in the 1925 earthquake."*
W.R. McGee

NP 5102, after having been fitted with roller bearings, at Livingston on 10-25-40. The first four of these locomotives (5100, 5101, 5102, and 5103) had friction bearings on all drivers when built and didn't perform as well as the rest. All four were converted to roller bearings during their first trip to the shops. *W.R. McGee*

Westbound Extra 5107 near Muir, Montana on 11-1-40. *"Just out of the Livingston shops after being slicked up."* R.V. Nixon

Two views of NP 5111 on 1-25-41.
In the top photo, the engine is
seen at Livingston as it is just about
to begin its run. In the lower view,
the train is photographed some
three miles west of Livingston.
R.V. Nixon

Train No. 602 with NP 5102 on the Low Line through the Gallatin Valley near Belgrade, Montana on 1-26-41. This is the point where the Low Line crosses the High Line. In the background are the Bridger Mountains. *W.R. McGee*

NP 5107 and Train No. 602 (3,857 tons) along the Missouri River at Brewer, Montana on 3-6-41. *W.R. McGee*

Here are three views of NP 5108 and the second section of Train No. 1, a fourteen car Army Special. Both Ron and Warren were out photographing this run on 3-7-41. In the upper left photo, the train has just passed through Hoppers Tunnel and is eight miles west of Livingston. This tunnel was day-lighted in the summer of 1951 and the double track was removed in 1957. The lower view was taken in Rocky Canyon near Chestnut, Montana. The location of the photograph on the facing page was a vantage point three miles west of Livingston. After 1936, the Z-6's were frequently assigned to the North Coast Limited between Livingston and Missoula when they were running thirteen or more cars. This usually occurred during the winter months between September and April. Engine's 5110 and 5111 got the assignment more often than any of the other Z-6's.

Upper left & right: W.R. McGee
Lower left: R.V. Nixon

The west end of Hoppers Tunnel proved to be a favorite spot of the photographers for capturing the NP's trains. The top photo is of NP 5108 and the Second No. 1 on 3-7-41. The lower view is of Extra 5101, taken one day later. *R.V. Nixon*

Train No. 603, with NP 1825, 5117, and 107 cars (5,025 tons), climbing out of the Columbia River Valley, three miles west of Kennewick, Washington on 5-5-41. We'll follow this train over the next few pages as it makes its way towards its destination. *W.R. McGee*

At left, Train No. 603 is now steaming along the Yakima River near Chandler, Washington. The helper has been cut off and the 5117 will continue to take it the rest of the way to Yakima. *"This train will be split in two at Yakima before proceeding to Auburn. The first section will contain all the hot merchandise loads (38 cars) and will be pulled by W-3 1829. Class Z-3 4017 will handle the second section. The first section will arrive in Auburn three hours before the second one."* In the photo above, the train is photographed as it approaches Gibbon, Washington. *W.R. McGee*

Now photographed approaching Union Gap, Washington, Train No. 603 looms over the now vintage autos on U.S. Highway 97. *W.R. McGee*

162

Westbound Extra 5120 at the NP-Milwaukee Road interchange point in front of the NP's Lombard, Montana depot on 9-3-41. The GE Motors and the depot in the background, as well as the bridge over the Missouri River from which this photo was taken, belong to the Milwaukee Road. There have been no buildings of any kind here since 1968. *W.R. McGee*

NP 5117, just out of the shops, at Livingston on 11-13-41. *"On a Z-6 you would run out of water before you ran out of coal. When the Z-6's first arrived they held 20,000 gallons of water, but there was a bulkhead in the back of the tender which had room for 2,000 gallons more. They wanted to see if the weight of the water would be excessive on the axles of the tender. Once they decided there was no danger of running hot, they knocked a hole in the bulkhead. After that they held 22,000 gallons. This was still not enough, so when the Z-7's came, they were designed to hold 25,000 gallons."* W.R. McGee

Westbound 5118 departs on the viaduct through Spokane, Washington on 8-11-43. *W.R. McGee*

Train No. 603 with NP 5108 and 5110 rolls west with seventy-eight cars (3,400 tons) at Elton Bluffs, Montana on 4-30-52. Double heading of Challengers mainly occured to balance power when an engine was needed on another part of the system. *"The engineer in the rear engine told me that he shoved the first engine all the way from Laurel. The guy in front didn't like going fast. You had fast engineers and slow engineers."* W.R. McGee

Westbound 5114 with seventy-two cars at Ritzville, Washington on 10-1-53.
W.R. McGee

Train No. 1 with NP 5101 arriving at Missoula, Montana on 7-22-54. *"The 5101 was a lemon. When I was dispatching I hated to see it on the train sheet as it usually meant trouble."* R.V. Nixon

Extra 5100-5120 eastbound near Bearmouth, Montana on 5-27-54. *"It was against the rules to double-head Z-6 engines. When I was dispatching I had instructions not to do it. I don't know how they got away with it here. There were several reasons for avoiding it; a lot of concentrated weight, too much binding on sharp curves, and a chance of derailing the second engine."* The 5100 was the first Z-6 built, 5120 the last. *R.V. Nixon*

CLASS Z-7

ALCO	4-6-6-4
Built:	1941
6 Engines	5121-5126

Westbound Extra 5121 at Toston, Montana on 11-15-41. *"This is the first picture of a Z-7 in service. It was set up at Livingston and left at night. This photo was taken before sunrise. Sort of a test train, mechanical officials rode in the coach and the superintendent's private car was coupled in behind it. I rode in the super's car and it was rough! The 5121 kept slipping."* R. V. Nixon

NP 5121 awaits clearance of eastbound 5101 at Toston, Montana before continuing its first revenue run. *R.V. Nixon*

Extra 5121 westbound with 5,650 tons leaving Laurel Yard on 11-20-41.
"This new engine was supposed to pull the world, but it took fifteen hours to go the hundred miles to Livingston, and they had to reduce the tonnage twice." W.R. McGee

171

Two views of NP 5122 packing 4,227 tons on its first revenue trip east of Livingston - at Mission, Montana on the left, at Columbus, Montana on the right. Warren McGee was the brakeman for this run on 11-22-41. *W.R. McGee*

Train No. 603 westbound with NP 5122 and sixty-four cars (3,464 tons) at the Greycliff, Montana coal dock on 11-25-41. *"The tenders on the Z-7's held twenty-five thousand gallons of water and twenty-seven tons of coal. You would run out of both at the same time, whereas on the Z-6's, you would run out of water first. Without stopping for fuel, a good run with a Z-7 at full throttle would last from two hours and twenty minutes to two hours and twenty-seven minutes."* W.R. McGee

Extra 5121 eastbound with 3,702 tons, heading into the siding at Big Timber,
Montana on 11-26-41. *W.R. McGee*

Eastbound No. 602 with NP 5121 and Helper 4503 at the foot of the 1.9% mountain grade of Bozeman Pass on 11-29-41. *W.R. McGee*

Now three miles west of Bozeman Pass, Train No. 602 is photographed near
Chestnut, Montana. *W.R. McGee*

NP 5126 leaving the coal dock at Livingston on 12-28-41. *W.R. McGee*

NP 5123 on its first trip, at
Livingston on 12-5-41. *R. V. Nixon*

Westbound NP 5125 arriving at
Missoula on 4-11-43. *R. V. Nixon*

Eastbound 5123 leaving Missoula on 7-19-43. *"This was the longest passenger train I recall seeing, thirty-two Pullmans."* R. V. Nixon

Westbound NP 5121 at Muir, Montana on 7-28-45. This was the first train to enter the new Bozeman Tunnel. *R. V. Nixon*

NP 5121 breaks the tape as the first train through the new Bozeman Tunnel on 7-28-45. "You have to begin a shortage of fuel as you near the tunnel, to burn all of the gases out of your coal. When you go into the tunnel all you want to have is heat and very little gas. It's a long mile through it and coal gas will kill you." W.R. McGee

Third No. 2 with NP 5123 at Missoula, Montana on 9-27-45. Note the interesting army transport cars. *R. V. Nixon*

Westbound 5126 and 125 cars along the Missouri River at Lombard Curve, Montana on 7-28-47. *"You can't get into this area at all. I was fifteen years getting delayed in a siding long enough so I could walk up and get a picture of the train coming the opposite direction. Even then I was nearly left there and just did manage to get back on fifteen cars back. This area was nothing but rocks and rattlesnakes. Eight hundred people lived there in 1907 and a circus even came to town in 1916. Today not one building remains. Lombard was also the western terminal of the Montana Railroad."* W.R. McGee

Two views of eastbound NP 5121 with Train No. 602 about to enter
Mullan Tunnel at Blossburg, Montana on 9-27-54. Blossburg is located
on the Continental Divide, 5,548 feet above sea level. Diesel power
replaced steam on this section on 11-6-54. *W.R. McGee*

NP 5141's first run, at Missoula, Montana on 4-18-43. *R. V. Nixon*

CLASS Z-8

20 Engines	4-6-6-4
5130-5141	ALCO 1943
5142-5149	ALCO 1944

Eastbound 5140, the "J" Manifest, at Thompson Falls, Montana on 9-17-45. *R.V. Nixon*

NP 5141 with a refrigerator special at Spring Gulch, Montana on 3-1-46. *R.V. Nixon*

NP 5133 at Bozeman, Montana on 3-9-47. *W.R. McGee*

188

Train No. 602 with NP 5132, seventy-seven loads, six empties, and NP 5126 helping on the 1.8% grade at Blossburg, Montana on 5-30-48. *W.R. McGee*

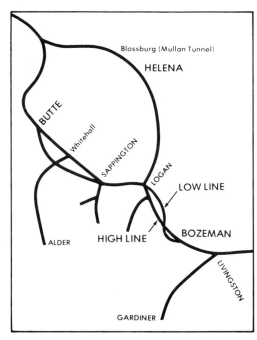

Two views of westbound NP 5132 with ninety cars (2,070 tons) on the Butte Line near Logan, Montana on 3-17-49. Due to a cave-in at Mullan Tunnel on the Helena Line fifteen days earlier, the Butte Line became the mainline until repairs were completed on 12-6-49. Siding capacities limited trains to ninety cars on this line. *W.R. McGee*

HIGH LINE-LOW LINE

The 1% grade out of Logan was one of the reasons for construction in 1919 of the Low Line between Logan and Bozeman. The Low Line provided an easier grade for eastbound freights, but was nine miles longer. The High Line was the mainline and carried all passenger trains and westbound freights.

Eastbound 5136-5147, the "J" Manifest, with sixty-three loads and twenty-four empties, two miles east of Springdale, Montana on 11-20-50. *W.R. McGee*

NP 5137 with the second section of Train No. 1, an eleven car Army Special, in Hangman Creek Canyon (Spokane area) on 9-25-52. *W.R. McGee*

NP 5145 at Parkwater (Spokane), Washington on 9-27-52. This engine was built in 1944 and scrapped at South Tacoma just eleven years later on 6-10-55. The ledger value was $276,550, the scrap value $13,977. *W.R. McGee*

Eastbound 5146, the "J" Manifest, with forty-three loads and fifteen empties
(2,800 tons), along the Yellowstone River at Springdale, Montana on 11-17-42.
W.R. McGee

Westbound Extra 5139, east of Hope, Idaho on 6-24-52. The NP was occasionally forced to use the Milwaukee Road's tracks through this area due to flooding and washouts on their own line. *R.V. Nixon*

Westbound Extra 5144, a special ribbon rail train, photographed west of Eddy, Montana on 7-12-53. *R.V. Nixon*

NP 5134 alongside the coal dock at Helena, Montana on 10-19-53. *W.R. McGee*

Helper 5131 lends some assistance to the westbound NP 5130 on the 1.8%
Bozeman Pass grade at Muir, Montana on 10-1-54. Diesels took over on this
line a little over a month later. *W.R. McGee*

NP 5130 helping Train No. 1 over Marent Trestle on 11-17-54. At 226 feet, Marent Trestle was the NP's tallest. At one time, nothing heavier than a W-3 was allowed to cross it. *R.V. Nixon*

Eastbound 5134 arriving at Missoula Yard on 3-4-55. *"This is the engine that derailed on a curve near Logan at about ninety miles per hour."* R.V. Nixon

EMC GAS ELECTRICS

EMC	St. Louis Car (body)
Built : 1925-1930	23 Cars
B-3 - B-26	(2 B-6's, no B-25)

Gas Electric B-18, Train No. 4's connection, at Lombard, Montana on 3-21-49. Mullan Tunnel had caved in and No. 4 was running by way of Butte. *W.R. McGee*

Branch line Gas Electric B-21 awaiting connection at Mandan, North Dakota on 8-3-38. Train No. 3 with NP 2236 is alongside. *W.R. McGee*

Northern Pacific B-11 at Jamestown, North Dakota on 8-25-50. *R.V. Nixon*

NP 1049 on the turntable at the Parkwater Shops at Spokane, Washington on 4-18-40. The mainrod drives the number two driver on L-9's 1040-1049. On the rest of the L-9's it was the number three driver. *W.R. McGee*

CLASS L-9

ALCO & Baldwin	0-6-0
Built:	1906-1910
95 Engines	1040-1134

CLASS S-4

Baldwin	4-6-0
Built:	1902
40 Engines	1350-1389

Eastbound Extra 1359, the Coeur d'Alene Local, crosses the Spokane River near Irvin, Washington on 6-24-52. *R. V. Nixon*

NP Switcher 1176 adding SP&S cars to Train No. 4 at Pasco, Washington on 6-5-46. *R. V. Nixon*

CLASS G-2		
ALCO		0-8-0
Built:		1920
20 Engines		1174-1193

An unusual and unposed shot of four different NP class engines at Livingston on 7-1-41. Left to right: 2667 (incoming on No. 1), 1529 (outgoing on No. 217), 2232 (outgoing on No. 1), and 4503 (an incoming helper). During the summer months when the North Coast Limited (Train No. 1) arrived in two sections, it was the herder's job to change the power on both sections, then take the incoming engine back to the roundhouse. NP 4503 was a helper that had just come back of the hill and was forced to wait its turn returning to the roundhouse. *R.V. Nixon*

The old Bozeman Tunnel was too confining for the Z-5 class 2-8-8-4's, so they built a new one. Here the track gang is moving the mainline over to begin operation of the new tunnel on 7-28-45. The new Bozeman Tunnel is 3,015 feet long, single track, and was built at a cost of $1,250,000. The old tunnel, built in 1883, saw its last train go through on this day. *W.R. McGee*

This is how it looked at the Livingston yards on 5-26-46 during the nation-wide railroad strike. The North Coast Limited was the only train the NP operated and it was pulled by diesel freight power. *W.R. McGee*

A birds-eye view of the Livingston yards and shop area on New Years Day, 1949. These were the NP's main shops west of the Mississippi. All the major work on the Challengers and Yellowstones was done here. *W.R. McGee*

A Few Notes On The Yellowstone Park Line

Of all the national parks, Yellowstone is the most universal in its appeal. The Northern Pacific, established early in 1872, became the first railroad to service a national park in 1883. The Yellowstone Park Line was the most publicized branchline on the railroad. It created thousands of tourists for the park and created positive public relations for the railroad. From about 1900 through 1953, "Yellowstone Park Line" appeared below the NP logo and on all promotion and advertising literature, china and other dinner items, timetables, and observation car tail signs. For many years the NP published a booklet "Wonderland", which was the NP nickname for Yellowstone Park.

Gardiner, Montana, which opened in 1883, was the beginning of the dramatic Yellowstone tour. The Gardiner Gateway Arch, made of basaltic rock, was dedicated by President Theodore Roosevelt in 1903. Over the center, carved in rustic letters, is the inscription *"For The Benefit And Enjoyment Of The People".* Service to Gardiner was maintained by the NP from June 10 thru September 15, the park vacation season. The route via Livingston was a scenic fifty-four mile trip along the Yellowstone River, with the Absaroka Mountains to the east, and the Gallatin Mountains to the west.

The Northern Pacific offered many package tours of Yellowstone. The most popular was a six day tour, which began with arrival at Livingston and proceeded with the ride to Gardiner. From there the passengers boarded tour busses and were treated to such sights as Gardiner Gateway, Mammoth Springs, Old Faithful, Yellowstone Lake, and the Grand Canyon of the Yellowstone. Lodging at the Old Faithful Inn and Grand Canyon Hotel was also included.

A short-lived, little known train was the Yellowstone Comet, which operated from about 1926 to 1929. The Comet was a CB&Q-Northern Pacific summertime train which ran between Chicago and Yellowstone Park. During the summer months the NP usually ran two sections of the North Coast Limited and Alaskan between St. Paul and Livingston. The Yellowstone Comet was just a special name, an advertising gimmick, for the second section of the North Coast Limited westbound, and the second section of the Alaskan eastbound. The same held true for the Livingston to Gardiner trains, No. 2 in the morning and No. 234 in the evening. The train numbers were the same with or without the Comet. The Comet served all of the principle gateways to Yellowstone. It carried Pullmans from Chicago direct to Gardiner, others direct to Cody, Wyoming, and still others direct to Bozeman and the new Gallatin Gateway. The buses of the Yellowstone Park Transportation Company made direct connections at these gateways. It was the same way leaving the park. A tourist was not limited to using the same gateway entering and leaving. The Comet died with the Depression, but the same park services were provided after its demise.

The Northern Pacific will always be remembered for its close relationship with Yellowstone Park.

Chapter 9

Yellowstone Park Line

Extra 1522, a Veteran's Special, at Gardiner, Montana on 6-17-40. The Northern Pacific was the first railroad to service a national park, beginning runs to Yellowstone in 1883. The archway in the upper right of the picture notes the original entrance to the park. Its cornerstone was laid by President Roosevelt in 1902. *"I was born about a block beyond where the first open observation car is located."* R.V. Nixon

NP 1530 with the three car Yellowstone Park Train No. 205 at Red Lodge,
Montana on 9-2-39. *"The NP provided bus service from Red Lodge to Cooke
City over the Cooke City Highway. This sixty-two mile highway was finished
in 1936 and reached an elevation of 10,942 feet. It was one of the first million
dollar highways in Montana and Wyoming."* W.R. McGee

Train No. 218 at Gardiner, Montana on 9-7-40. The Gardiner depot was made out of logs and was designed, as was the gateway arch, by architect Robert C. Reamer. He was also responsible for the Old Faithful Inn and the Lake Canyon Hotel inside the park. Sepulchre Mountain can be seen in the background. *R.V. Nixon*

Train No. 217 with NP 1529 north of Gardiner on 9-12-40. 11,555 foot high Electric Peak is in the background. *"This is one of the last Yellowstone Park trains, which in earlier years, consisted of from ten to sixteen cars. Note the open air observation car. In the 1920's, two of them were used on each train."* R.V. Nixon

Westbound NP 2119, a Civilian Conservation Corps Special, leaving Livingston on 11-14-41. *"This may have been the last steam powered passenger train to run on this line. Warren McGee's father was the engineer."* Ninety pound rail was used for ten miles at the southern end of this line, the rest of it was seventy-two pound rail. It carried a twenty-five mile per hour speed limit until its demise in 1976. *R.V. Nixon*

Train No. 234 with NP 1902 near Gardiner on 9-12-40. The Yellowstone
River can be seen in the background. *R.V. Nixon*

Train No. 217 with NP 1529 and 2152 along the Yellowstone River, about thirty-five miles south of Livingston, on 7-16-41. This view was taken from the Yellowstone Trail, with Yankee Jim's Canyon in the distance and Tom Miner's Basin off to the right. *W.R. McGee*

216

Train No. 217 now arriving at Gardiner. *"The lead engine on the Yellowstone Park train was usually an oil burner, the second engine usually a coal burner. Two open air observation cars were run on this train, referred to as 'rubber neck cars' by the crew. The three cars behind them are standard sleepers, full of tourists arriving to ride buses through the park. At the rear of the train rode the Civilian Conservation Corps boys, on their way to work in the park. A freight train went up this line twice a week, passenger trains ran daily. The freight trains had usually completed switching and were already gone by the time the passenger train arrived."* W.R. McGee

Two more views of Train No. 217 at Gardiner on 7-16-41. Only one engine was needed to make the return trip back downgrade to Livingston, so the 2152 will be cut off here and return light. *W.R. McGee*

NP 6509, the first and only passenger diesel to run on this line, with ten cars at Gardiner on 9-8-53. *"I was the conductor on this train, with car loads of farmers from Indiana and Michigan."* W.R. McGee

General Motors No. 103 test train arriving at Missoula, Montana on 3-16-40. GM 103 was the prototype for the first group of mass produced diesel freight locomotives in the United States. They filled out this train to seventeen cars in Livingston to see if this 5,400 horsepower four-unit FT would be able to pull it up the mountain. *"I asked my dad if I could use his brand new Nash to go up to Muir, about twenty miles away, and take pictures of this thing. I ended up 120 miles away in Butte, just like all kids I guess! The diesel made up thirteen minutes on Butte Mountain's 2.2% grade. It just loafed along and made fun of those hills. This run marked the beginning of a new era of locomotion."* (W.R. McGee story) R.V. Nixon

GM FT No. 103	
EMD	Built 1939
4 Units	1350 Horsepower
Dk. Green w/Yellow Stripes	

The North Coast Limited with GM 103 near Turah, Montana on 3-18-40. This was the first trip for the NCL under diesel power. Immediately behind the diesel was Dynamometer Car No. 276, then four business cars full of brass hats, then the remainder of the regular NCL for a total of seventeen cars. *"It was quite a historic trip as this was the first time a train of that size was handled from Livingston to Missoula without a helper. The GM 103 made the round trip in one day, maintaining the NCL's schedule."* R.V. Nixon

GM 754

GM 754 test train, all ready to go, at St. Paul, Minnesota on 11-2-46. This three unit diesel was built during F-2 production in 1946 and was used to demonstrate F-3 performance for passenger service. *W.R. McGee*

General Motors No. 754 arriving at Livingston with an eleven car test train on 11-3-46. This train will be displayed here for three hours. *"I was the head brakeman on this train. The Billings to Livingston run was scheduled for one hour and forty-one minutes, we took one hour fifty-two, and in later years Amtrak set a schedule of one hour thirty-nine. The run between Livingston and Butte was set for two hours and fifty-five minutes and was easier to accomplish. We killed nine* *minutes standing still at Homestake, arriving in Butte at four-thirty that afternoon. The Great Northern and the Milwaukee Road ran faster schedules by bussing Southern Montana passengers north to Roundup and Ringling to board the Milwaukee's No. 15 and 16. Five years later on 11-16-52, the NP instituted a competitive thirty-nine hour schedule and took most of the Milwaukee's business from this area."* W.R. McGee

GM 754 on display at Livingston with the first of the new coaches. *"All the way across the division we were flagged by the section hands and everybody was kept clear. We were given a free hand to run at the engineers judgement. The speed limit through Whitehall was normally thirty-five miles per hour, but on that day we went through there at seventy. It was okay at the head end of the train in the new coaches, but the ride in the older cars at the end of the train was pretty rough. The rear brakeman got so nervous he laid down in the aisle because he thought they were going to tip over. Of course these older cars were full of brass hats too. We gave them a real thrill."* (W.R. McGee story) R.V. Nixon

GM 754 at Homestake, Montana on 11-3-46. The trip from St. Paul to Seattle took thirty-three hours and fifty-six minutes. *R. V. Nixon*

Brand new NP 6504 awaiting its first trip, at St. Paul, Minnesota on 1-26-47.
R. V. Nixon

CLASS F-3

EMD	A-B-B
Built:	1947
7 Sets	6500-6506

NP 6500 at St. Paul on 1-20-47.
This photo was taken before it had
made a trip. *R. V. Nixon*

Train No. 6 with NP 6502 and
2626 at Seattle on 7-25-53.
R. V. Nixon

Class F-3 6505, with the sixteen car North Coast Limited, on its first run from
St. Paul to Seattle, photographed five miles west of Livingston on 2-2-47.
While the NCL used only fifteen percent of the NP's passenger cars, it
accounted for nearly half of the railroad's passenger train income. *W.R. McGee*

NP 6502 with the North Coast Limited at Missoula on 4-28-47. *W.R. McGee*

The North Coast Limited with NP 6510 crosses Marent Trestle on 6-10-50.
This bridge is located seventeen miles west of Missoula. *R. V. Nixon*

The North Coast Limited with NP 6506 leaving St. Paul on 6-3-50. *R. V. Nixon*

NP 6506 and the North Coast Limited on the trestle near Skones, Montana on 5-24-49. *"A lot of stories could be written about this trestle. The track is carved through volcanic rock with the floor of the valley about a thousand feet below. Descending trains would hit the trestle at a high rate of speed and I often heard women in the vista-dome scream when the train apparently took off into thin air."* R. V. Nixon

The North Coast Limited with NP 6503 at Fargo, North Dakota on 3-30-50.
R.V. Nixon

Train No. 311 with NP 501 near Marshall, Washington in August of 1951. Not all of the NP's passenger trains got streamlined F units. *R.V. Nixon*

Train No. 26 with NP 6506 and eleven cars at Springdale, Montana on 11-21-52. Warren McGee's father was the engineer on this train. *W.R. McGee*

Train No. 26 with NP 6500 and eleven cars (but no vista-domes) along the Yellowstone River near Springdale, Montana on 8-17-53. *W.R. McGee*

NP 6504 with the sixteen car Mainstreeter leaving Spokane, Washington on 10-2-53. Northern Pacific numbering practice became confusing following purchase of the F-7 units. Convention was to assign units a locomotive set number such as 6504A - 6504B - 6504C above. Notice that 6504C is an F-7A while on page 227, 6504C is an F-3B. Before arrival of the F-7's, locomotives were assigned in A-B-B configuration while afterward F-3 and F-7 units were interchangeably assembled in A-B-A configuration with unit numbers changed to match the locomotive set number. Forty-eight F-7 freight units were numbered in the 6007 - 6020 series. *W.R. McGee*

CLASS F-7

EMD	A-B-A
Built:	1949-1950
21 Units	6500-6513, 6550
(see explanation, page 236)	

The North Coast Limited at Elton Bluffs, Montana on 8-17-53. The NP bought three F-7 A-B-A sets, plus enough extra cab units to convert the original F-3 A-B-B sets into A-B-A sets. The second car back on this train was one of the first to be painted in the new Loewy color scheme. *"The 1947 color scheme was changed to the Loewy scheme in 1953 because the NP received a new president between those years and he wanted a different image."* W.R. McGee

Train No. 25 leaving the yard at Missoula on 7-16-54. *R. V. Nixon*

No. 552, the first dome to go west, at Paradise, Montana on 7-27-54. The NP added the lettering "Vista Dome North Coast Limited" to the sides of these cars in 1957. Similar lettering went on the sides of the lounges, diners, and observation cars as well.
R.V. Nixon

Train No. 25 with NP 6500 arriving at Butte on 8-19-54. "The Richest Hill on Earth" is in the background. At left is the old Montana Union Roundhouse.
R.V. Nixon

NP President Macfarlane on the platform of his private car, the Yellowstone
River, at Missoula on 3-20-55. *"When President Macfarlane bought those three
private cars, (the Clark Fork River and the Missouri River were the other two)
they were the most expensive passenger cars that had ever been built. The bill
for each of these three cars averaged out to $346,666. Prior to that time, the
most expensive passenger cars were those full length domes that the Milwaukee
Road built for their Olympian Hiawatha. They cost $331,000 apiece. That was
the kind of money the NP had in those days."* (W.R. McGee story)
R.V. Nixon photo

Train No. 25 with NP 6507 leaving Missoula on 6-13-55. This view captures an interesting mixture of equipment in the yard area. In the lower lefthand corner is one of the NP's standard wood cabooses. They rebuilt the end platforms and ladders on these beginning in 1940. Monad's (the NP logo) were first applied to the cabooses around May of 1951. A couple of steel cabooses can also be seen along with NP 33 (a Y class 2-8-0, which can not have many days left), and a Class S-2 diesel switcher No. 712.
R.V. Nixon

Train No. 25 at Missoula on 6-15-55.
R.V. Nixon

At left, the eastbound NP 6504 crosses the S bridge on the Wallace Branch on 7-18-58. This was the last passenger train to run over this line. *"Note that there are no railings on this trestle."*
R.V. Nixon

At right, Train No. 25 with NP 6506 and thirteen cars is photographed along the Yellowstone River at Milepost 99 on 6-19-55. This spot is about sixteen miles east of Livingston. *W.R. McGee*

The NP's Gyro Special at Wallace, Idaho on 4-1-58. This was a one time
only run between Wallace and Taft as part of a service organization
celebration. *R.V. Nixon*

Westbound NP 6001 at Blossburg, Montana on 4-12-44. This was the first road diesel to operate west of Livingston on the NP. *"They were assigned to the Yellowstone Division just long enough to avoid the Washington sales tax. This picture was used on the joker of the NP's playing cards."* R.V. Nixon

CLASS FT

EMD	A-B-B-A
Built:	1944-1945
11 Sets	6000-6010

Eastbound NP 6003 at Maywood, Washington on 2-9-45. In January of 1950 these engines were renumbered to 5400 series to reflect the horsepower of each set (5,400 horsepower). *R.V. Nixon*

NP 6003 helping out the steam powered North Coast Limited over Stampede
Pass at Martin, Washington on 2-11-45. *"Sort of a deceptive picture, but the
NP's advertising department was pleased with it. The NP didn't have any
passenger diesels at the time. The seven bulb headlight was a factory option."*
R.V. Nixon

Train No. 4 with NP 6008 and 2248 near Stampede, Washington on 3-31-45. *"Snowing heavily although it doesn't show in the picture. I stepped off the diesel into about two feet of snow."* R.V. Nixon

Eastbound Train No. 602 with NP 6010 and ninety-seven cars (5,073 tons) along the Missouri River near Lombard, Montana on 7-28-47. *"I was fifteen years getting to this place walking, as there are no roads within three miles of this point. A 3,000 foot tunnel was once contemplated that would have eliminated this curve and five miles of very crooked track. The tunnel proposal was denied however, because of fear of striking large underground streams."* W.R. McGee

Train No. 602 with NP 6001 descending the 2.2 percent grade at Homestake, Montana on 8-21-49. Engine 6005 is cut in behind sixty percent of the tonnage and will be dropped off at Whitehall. Warren's dad was in the cab of 6005.
W.R. McGee

CLASS F-9

GM	A-B-B-A
Built:	1954-1956
15 Sets	7000-7014

NP 7001, a brand new four unit set, at Livingston on 2-4-54. *"Of all the diesel power that the NP employed, the 7000 series F-9's were the first to convince most of the railroad men that they really had something. These engines produced more power and were such a contrast from the FT's, that it was like going from a Model T to a Cadillac. A three unit F-7 set was just about equivalent to a mallet (4,500 horsepower), but with four of these F-9's you could really move a train. Leaving Laurel westbound with our regular train of 5,500 tons under steam power took twelve miles just to get up to forty miles per hour. With these new diesels, we were up to fifty-five in just four miles. They could handle 4,4000 tons up the 2.2% Helena to Blossburg grade all by themselves."* By April of 1955, the entire Rocky Mountain Division of the NP was dieselized. *W.R. McGee*

Brand new NP 7000 at Missoula, Montana on 4-18-54. *R.V. Nixon*

Westbound NP 501 at Marshall, Washington on 4-13-51. The NP had two of these engines; they were originally intended for passenger service. At first numbered 175 and 176, they were renumbered in December of 1949. *R. V. Nixon*

CLASS DRS-4-4-1500

Baldwin	1948
2 Engines	500-501

NP 3601 at Paradise, Montana on 7-15-64. *"When the NP wanted pictures of their new diesels, I always tried to catch them at Paradise because of the background." R.V. Nixon*

CLASS SD-45

EMD	1966-1968
30 Engines	3600-3629

Train No. 652, with NP 311 and 273, west of Welch, Montana on 6-26-66.
"This is the only train still running on the Butte Line. The Burlington
Northern is planning on abandoning it altogether." R.V. Nixon

CLASS GP-9

EMD	1954-1958
176 Engines	200-375

Locomotive Index

The following is a list of the locomotives pictured in this book and the page numbers upon which they appear.

4012: 120
4017: 115, 116, 117
4021: 114, 119
4025: 113, 118, 119,
    121, 122, 123

Class Z-4
4500: 124, 138*, 146
4501: 140*
4503: 176*, 177*, 206

Yellowstone 2-8-8-4

Class Z-5
5000: 5, 129, 130
5003: 126, 128
5006: 125
5008: 127
5010: 126
5011: 131

Challengers 4-6-6-4

Class Z-6
5100: 138, 141, 168
5101: 158, 168, 170
5102: 151, 154
5103: 139, 208
5104: 146
5105: 134, 135, 142,
    143

5106: 144, 147, 148
5107: 53, 136, 140,
    149, 152, 155,
    rear end paper
5108: 156, 157, 158,
    166
5109: 150, 208
5110: 166
5111: 145, 153
5113: 134
5114: 134, 167
5115: 132, 134
5117: 137, 159, 160,
    161, 162, 164
5118: 165
5119: 137, 208
5120: 137, 149, 163,
    168

Class Z-7
5121: 169, 170, 171,
    175, 176, 177,
    180, 181, 184,
    185
5122: 172, 173, 174
5123: 179, 180, 182
5125: 179, 208
5126: 178, 183, 189*

Class Z-8
5130: 198*, 199

5131: 198
5132: 120*, 189, 190,
    191
5133: 188
5134: 197, 200
5136: 192
5137: 193
5139: 196
5140: 187
5141: 186, 187
5144: 196
5145: 194
5146: 195
5147: 192, 208

Miscellaneous

Gas Electrics
B-11: 202
B-18: 201
B-21: 202

Class L-9 0-6-0
1049: 203

Class G-2 0-8-0
1176: 205

Class S-4 4-6-0
1359: 204

Class Y 2-8-0
33: 241

Class Y-2 2-8-0
1269: 137
1276: 137

Diesels

Class FT
GM 103: 60, 221, 222
6000: 126*
6001: 245, 250
6003: 246, 247
6005: 250*
6008: 248
6010: 249

Class F-2
GM 754: 1, 3, 223, 224,
    225*, 226

Class F-3
6500: 199, 228, 235,
    239
6502: 228, 230
6503: 233
6504: 227, 236, 242,
    244
6505: 229
6506: 232, 234, 243

Class F-7
6507: 237, 241
6508: 3
6509: 220
6510: 231
6511: *ii*
6513: 10*

Class F-9
7000: 252
7001: 251

Class DRS-4-4-1500
501: 234, 253

Class GP-9
298: 242, 244
273: 255
311: 255

Class SD-45
3601: 254

Class S-2
712: 241

* At location, but
  not in photo.

Remaining NP Steam Locomotives

On Display

1	Minnetonka	0-4-0	Duluth, MN. - Lake Superior Museum of Transportation & Industry
10	Shop Locomotive	0-6-0	Brainerd, MN.
25	Y-1	2-8-0	Butte, MT.
684	C-1	4-4-0	Fargo, ND.
1031	L-7	0-6-0	Billings, MT.
1068	L-9	0-6-0	Dilworth, MN.
1354	S-4	4-6-0	Pasco, WA.
1356	S-4	4-6-0	Missoula, MT.
1382	S-4	4-6-0	Helena, MT.
2152	Q-3	4-6-2	Auburn, WA.
2153	Q-3	4-6-2	East Grand Forks, MN.
2164	Q-3	4-6-2	Bismark, ND.
2435	T	2-6-2	Duluth, MN. - Lake Superior Museum of Transportation & Industry
SP&S 539	O-3 (former NP W-3 1762)	2-8-2	Vancouver, WA.

Operating

328	S-10	4-6-0	St. Paul, MN. - Minnesota Transportation Museum
1070	L-9	0-6-0	Wickersham, WA. - Lake Whatcom Railway
2156	Q-3	4-6-2	Minneapolis, MN. - Being put in operating condition.

In Storage

924	L-5	0-6-0	Chehalis, WA. - Puget Sound Railway Historical Association
1364	S-4	4-6-0	Tacoma, WA. - Previously on display, but now in bad shape due to abandoned restoration attempt.

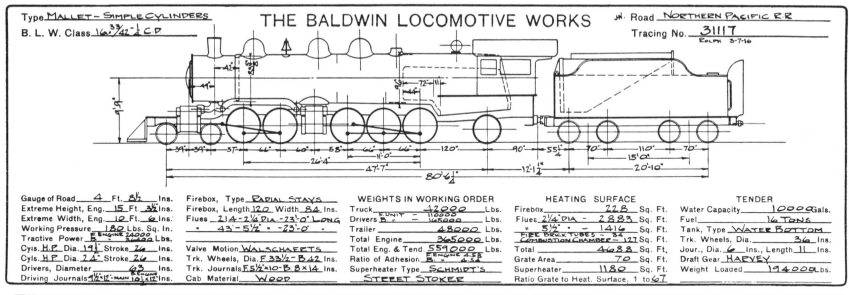

Type MALLET - SIMPLE CYLINDERS
B. L. W. Class 16⅜/42-¼ C.D

THE BALDWIN LOCOMOTIVE WORKS

Road NORTHERN PACIFIC R.R
Tracing No. 31117
ROLPH 3-7-16

Gauge of Road 4 Ft. 8½ Ins.	Firebox, Type RADIAL STAYS	WEIGHTS IN WORKING ORDER	HEATING SURFACE	TENDER
Extreme Height, Eng. 15 Ft. 3½ Ins.	Firebox, Length 120 Width 84 Ins.	Truck 42000 Lbs.	Firebox 228 Sq. Ft.	Water Capacity 10000 Gals.
Extreme Width, Eng. 10 Ft. 6 Ins.	Flues 214-2¼ DIA -23'-0" LONG	Drivers F.UNIT 110000 / B 165000 Lbs.	Flues 2¼ DIA - 2883 Sq. Ft.	Fuel 16 TONS
Working Pressure 180 Lbs. Sq. In.	" 43'-5½" - 23'-0'	Trailer 48000 Lbs.	" 5½ " - 1416 Sq. Ft.	Tank, Type WATER BOTTOM
Tractive Power F.ENGINE 24000 / 31200 Lbs.		Total Engine 365000 Lbs.	FIRE BRICK TUBES - 34 / COMBUSTION CHAMBER - 127 Sq. Ft.	Trk. Wheels, Dia. 36 Ins.
Cyls. H.P. Dia. 19½ Stroke 26 Ins.	Valve Motion WALSCHAERTS	Total Eng. & Tend. 559000 Lbs.	Total 4688 Sq. Ft.	Jour., Dia. 6 Ins., Length 11 Ins.
Cyls. H.P. Dia. 24" Stroke 26 Ins.	Trk. Wheels, Dia. F 33½-B 42 Ins.	Ratio of Adhesion F.ENGINE 4.58 / B 4.58	Grate Area 70 Sq. Ft.	Draft Gear HARVEY
Drivers, Diameter 63 Ins.	Trk. Journals F 5½×10-B 8×14 Ins.	Superheater Type SCHMIDT'S	Superheater 1180 Sq. Ft.	Weight Loaded 194000 Lbs.
Driving Journals 1½-12 -MAIN 10½×12 Ins.	Cab Material WOOD	STREET STOKER	Ratio Grate to Heat. Surface, 1 to 67	

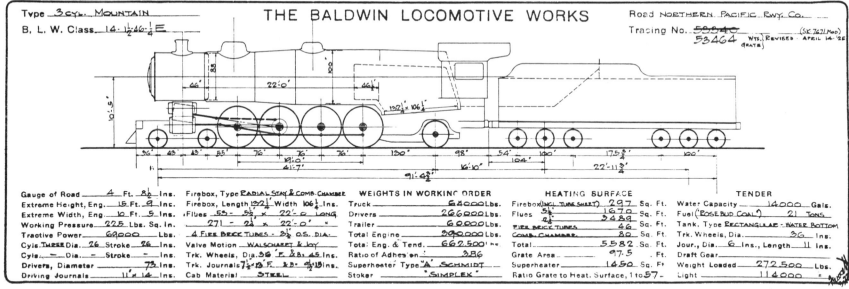

Type 3 CYL. MOUNTAIN
B. L. W. Class 14-1½-46-¼ E

THE BALDWIN LOCOMOTIVE WORKS

Road NORTHERN PACIFIC RWY. CO.
Tracing No. 53840 / 53464 (SK 7671 MOD) WTS. REVISED APRIL 14-'25 GRATE)

Gauge of Road 4 Ft. 8½ Ins.	Firebox, Type RADIAL STAY & COMB. CHAMBER	WEIGHTS IN WORKING ORDER	HEATING SURFACE	TENDER
Extreme Height, Eng. 15 Ft. 9 Ins.	Firebox, Length 132¼ Width 106¼ Ins.	Truck 64000 Lbs.	Firebox (INCL TUBE SHEET) 297 Sq. Ft.	Water Capacity 14000 Gals.
Extreme Width, Eng. 10 Ft. 5 Ins.	Flues 55 - 5½ × 22'-0 LONG	Drivers 266000 Lbs.	Flues 5½ 1670 / 2¼ 3489 Sq. Ft.	Fuel ("ROSE BUD COAL") 21 TONS
Working Pressure 225 Lbs. Sq. In.	271 - 2¼ × 22'-0' "	Trailer 60000 Lbs.	FIRE BRICK TUBES 46 Sq. Ft.	Tank, Type RECTANGULAR - WATER BOTTOM
Tractive Power 69000 Lbs.	4 FIRE BRICK TUBES - 8½ O.S. DIA.	Total Engine 390000 Lbs.	COMB. CHAMBER. 80 Sq. Ft.	Trk. Wheels, Dia. 36 Ins.
Cyls. THREE Dia. 26 Stroke 26 Ins.	Valve Motion WALSCHAERT & JOY	Total Eng. & Tend. 662500 Lbs.	Total 5582 Sq. Ft.	Jour., Dia. 6 Ins., Length 11 Ins.
Cyls. — Dia. — Stroke — Ins.	Trk. Wheels, Dia. 36 F. & B. 45 Ins.	Ratio of Adhesion 3.86	Grate Area 97.5 Sq. Ft.	Draft Gear
Drivers, Diameter 73 Ins.	Trk. Journals 7½×13 F. & B. 9×15 Ins.	Superheater Type "A" SCHMIDT	Superheater 1450 Sq. Ft.	Weight Loaded 272500 Lbs.
Driving Journals 11 × 14 Ins.	Cab Material STEEL	Stoker "SIMPLEX"	Ratio Grate to Heat. Surface, 1 to 57	Light 114000 "

BALDWIN PROPOSAL DRAWINGS

These drawings are for a pair of locomotives you won't find photographed in this book, as they were never actually built. Baldwin proposed these two in 1916 and 1925, but the NP went with ALCO designs instead. *(F.R. Martin collection)*

THE
NORTHERN PACIFIC RAILWAY

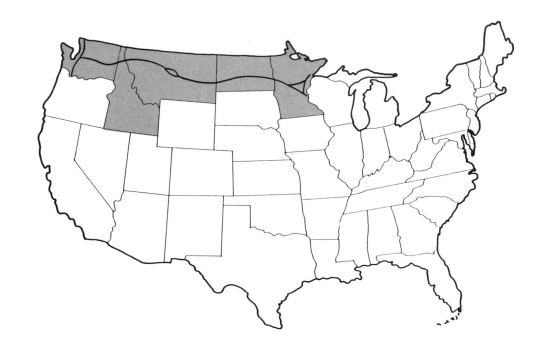

Route Maps And Photograph Locations

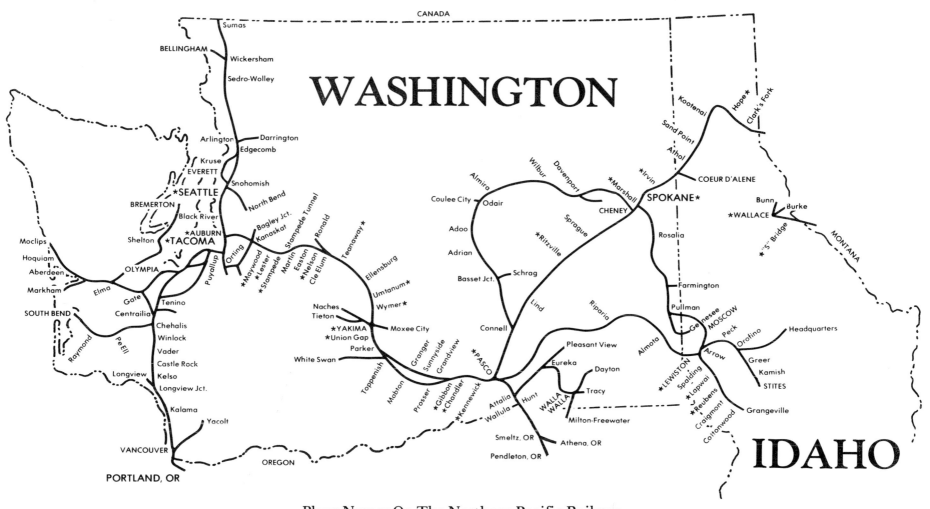

Place Names On The Northern Pacific Railway
Picture locations starred and referenced below.

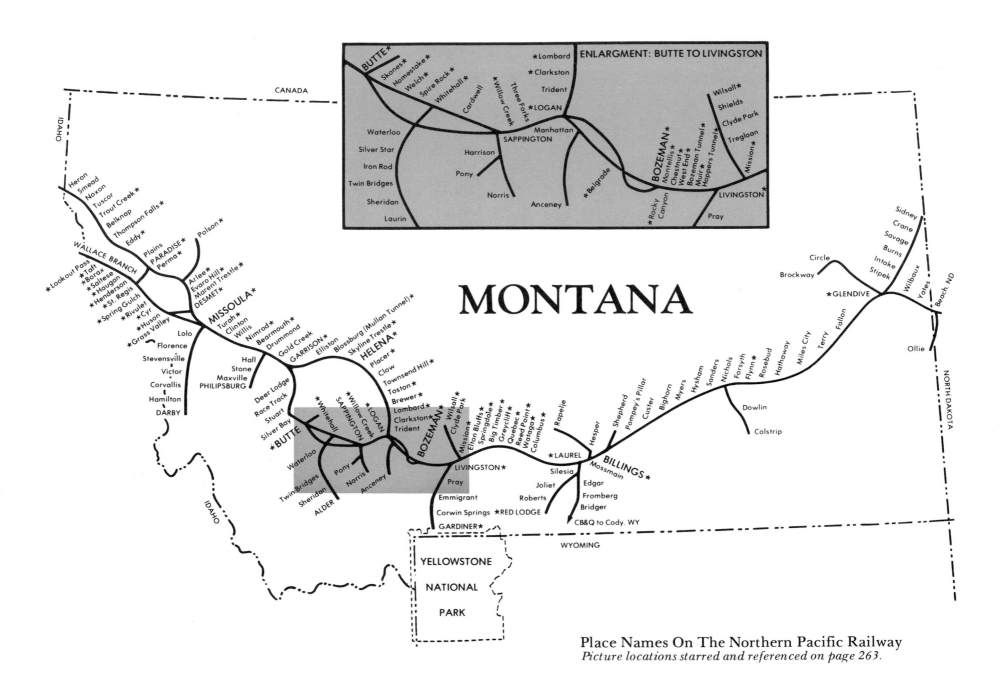

ENLARGMENT: BUTTE TO LIVINGSTON

BUTTE*

Skones*
Homestake*
Welch*
Spire Rock*
Whitehall*
Cardwell*
Willow Creek
Three Forks
*LOGAN

Lombard*
*Clarkston
Trident
Manhattan
SAPPINGTON

Wilsall*
Shields
Clyde Park
Tregloan*
Mission*

BOZEMAN*
Montellis*
Chestnut*
West End*
Bozeman Tunnel*
Hoppers Tunnel*

LIVINGSTON*

Waterloo
Silver Star
Iron Rod
Twin Bridges
Sheridan
Laurin

Harrison
Pony
Norris

Belgrade*

Anceney

*Rocky Canyon

Pray

CANADA

IDAHO

MONTANA

Heron
Smead
Noxon
Tuscor
Trout Creek*
Belknap
Thompson Falls*
Eddy*

Plains
PARADISE*
Perma*

Polson*

WALLACE BRANCH

Lookout Pass*
*Taft
*Borax
*Saltese
*Haugan
Henderson
*St. Regis
Spring Gulch*
*Rivulet
*Cyr
*Huson
*Grass Valley

Arlee*
Evaro Hill*
Marent Trestle*
DESMET*

MISSOULA*
Turah*
Clinton
Willis

Nimrod*
Bearmouth*
Drummond

Gold Creek
GARRISON*
Elliston

Blossburg (Mullan Tunnel)*
Skyline Trestle*

HELENA*
Placer*
Clow
Townsend Hill*
Toston*
Brewer*

Lolo
Florence
Stevensville
Victor
Corvallis
Hamilton
DARBY

Hall
Stone
Maxville
PHILIPSBURG

Deer Lodge
Race Track
Stuart
Silver Bay

BUTTE

*Willow Creek
SAPPINGTON*
LOGAN*
Lombard*
Clarkston*
Trident

Waterloo
Twin Bridges
Sheridan
ALDER

Pony
Norris
Anceney

*Whitehall

Wilsall*
Clyde Park*
Mission*
BOZEMAN*

Elton Bluffs*
Springdale*
Big Timber*
Greycliff*
Quebec*
Reed Point*
Wataga*
Columbus*

Rapelje

LIVINGSTON*
Pray
Emmigrant
Corwin Springs
GARDINER*

Silesia
Joliet
Roberts

*LAUREL

Hesper

Shepherd
Pompey's Pillar
Custer
Bighorn
Myers

Rapelje

Mossmain
BILLINGS*

Edgar
Fromberg
Bridger
CB&Q to Cody, WY

*RED LODGE

Hysham
Sanders
Nichols
Forsyth
Flynn
Rosebud
Hathaway
Miles City
Terry
Fallon

Dowlin
Colstrip

Circle
Brockway

Sidney
Crane
Savage
Burns
Intake
Stipek
Wilbaux
Yates

*GLENDIVE

Ollie

Beach, ND

NORTH DAKOTA

IDAHO

WYOMING

YELLOWSTONE

NATIONAL

PARK

Place Names On The Northern Pacific Railway
Picture locations starred and referenced on page 263.

Montana

Photograph locations
and page numbers:

Arlee: 46, 123

Bearmouth: 168
Belgrade: 154
Big Timber: 11, 175
Billings: 85
Blossburg: 184, 185, 189,
245
Borax: 35, 113, 119
Bozeman: 16, 39, 138, 188
Bozeman Tunnel: 17, 129,
207 (Also see Muir and
West End)
Brewer: 155
Butte: 3, 74, 239

Chestnut: 83, 136, 141,
148, 177
Clarkston: 42
Columbus: 173
Cyr: 33

DeSmet: 27

Eddy: 5, 63, 196
Elton Bluffs (Milepost
99): 166, 237, 243
Evaro Hill: 8, 26

Flynn: 105

Gardiner: 211, 213, 217,
218, 219, 220
North of Gardiner: 214,
215, 216
Garrison: 77
Glendive: 5, 44, 99, 110,
126
Grass Valley: 149
Greycliff: 15, 174

Haugan: 31, 114
Helena: 72, 197
Henderson: 121
Homestake: 226, 250
Hoppers Tunnel: 92,
120, 156, 158
Huson: 28

Laurel: 95, 171
Livingston: 1, 3, 29, 38,
47, 55, 56, 59, 62, 68,
71, 75, 87, 90, 94, 96,
97, 102, 104, 107, 108,
125, 128, 135, 142, 145,
151, 153, 164, 178, 179,
206, 208, 209, 214, 224
225, 251, Rear endpaper
West of Livingston: 63,
80, 91, 107, 124, 130,
146, 147, 153, 157, 229
Logan: 56, 66, 73, 101,
190, 191
Lombard: 64, 150, 163,
183, 201, 249
Lookout Pass: 121, 122

Marent Trestle: *iv*, 9,
18, 45, 199, 231
Mission: 172
Missoula: 7, 58, 60, 68,
168, 179, 180, 182, 186,
200, 221, 230, 238, 240,
241, 252
Montellis: 41

Muir: 13, 93, 143, 149,
152, 180, 181, 198

Nimrod: 61

Paradise: 50, 78, 109,
239, 254
Perma: 41
Placer: 139
Polson: 24

Quebec: 89

Red Lodge: 212
Reed Point: 20
Rivulet: 21, 30
Rocky Canyon: 40, 82,
140, 156, 176

Saltese: 123
Skones: 84, 232
Skyline Trestle: 65
Spire Rock: 8
Springdale: 192, 195,
234, 235
Spring Gulch: 187

St. Regis: 34, 118

Taft: 119
Thompson Falls: 187
Toston: 169, 170
Trident: 35, 48
Townsend Hill: 144
Trout Creek: 53
Turah: 222

Wataga: 127
Welch: 19, 43, 76, 80,
255
West End: 81, 134
Whitehall: 57, 91
Willow Creek: 67
Wilsall: 12

ELEVATIONS ALONG THE NP MAINLINE

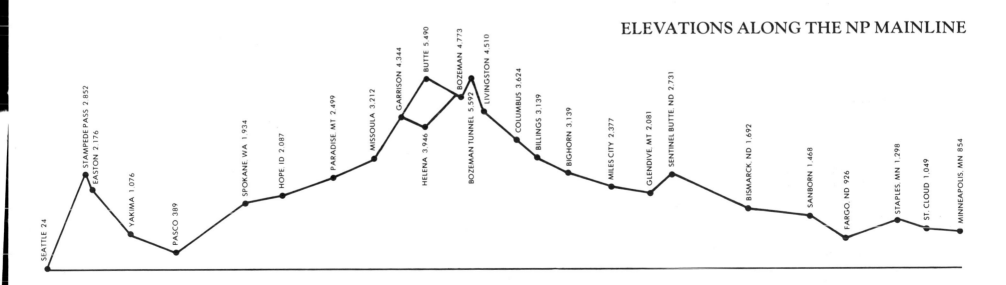

263

NORTH DAKOTA

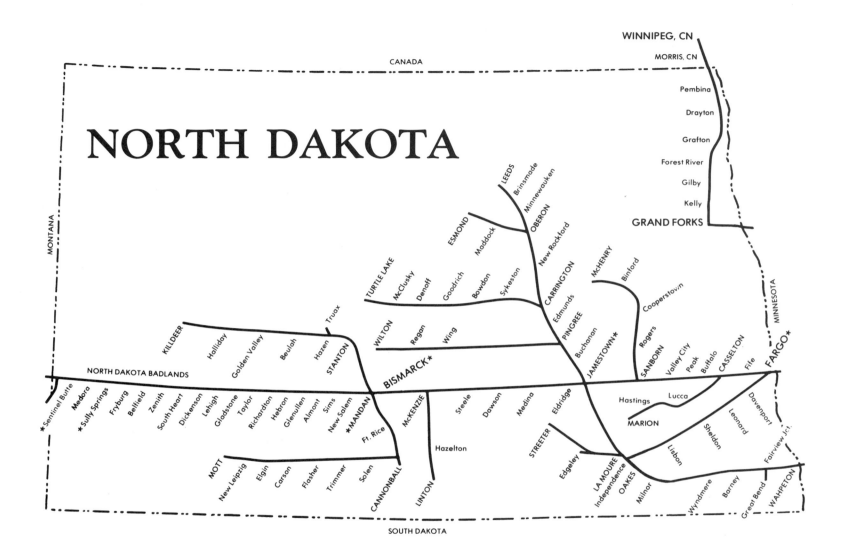

WINNIPEG, CN

MORRIS, CN

Pembina

Drayton

Grafton

Forest River

Gilby

Kelly

GRAND FORKS

CANADA

MONTANA

MINNESOTA

SOUTH DAKOTA

LEEDS

Brinsmade

Minnewauken

OBERON

New Rockford

ESMOND

Maddock

Goodrich

Bowdon

Sykeston

CARRINGTON

Edmunds

PINGREE

McHENRY

Binford

Cooperstown

TURTLE LAKE

McClusky

Denoff

Buchanan

JAMESTOWN*

Rogers

SANBORN

Valley City

Peak

Buffalo

CASSELTON

Fife

FARGO*

WILTON

Regan

Wing

Truax

KILDEER

Halliday

Golden Valley

Beulah

Hazen

STANTON

NORTH DAKOTA BADLANDS

BISMARCK*

Steele

Dawson

Medina

Eldridge

Hastings

Lucca

*Sentinel Butte

Medora

*Sully Springs

Fryburg

Belfield

Zenith

South Heart

Dickenson

Lehigh

Gladstone

Taylor

Richardton

Hebron

Glenullen

Almont

Sims

New Salem

*MANDAN

Ft. Rice

McKENZIE

MARION

Davenport

Leonard

Sheldon

Fairview Jct.

MOTT

New Leipzig

Elgin

Carson

Flasher

Trimmer

Solen

CANNONBALL

Hazelton

LINTON

STREETER

Edgeley

LA MOURE

Independence

OAKES

Milnor

Lisbon

Wyndmere

Barney

Great Bend

WAHPETON

Photograph locations and page numbers:

Bismarck: 37
Fargo: 233
Jamestown: 88, 98, 202
Mandan: 25, 202
Sentinel Butte: 126
Sully Springs: 131

Place Names On The Northern Pacific Railway
Picture locations starred and referenced at left.

Place Names On The Northern Pacific
Picture locations starred and referenced below.

Photograph locations
and page numbers:

MINNESOTA

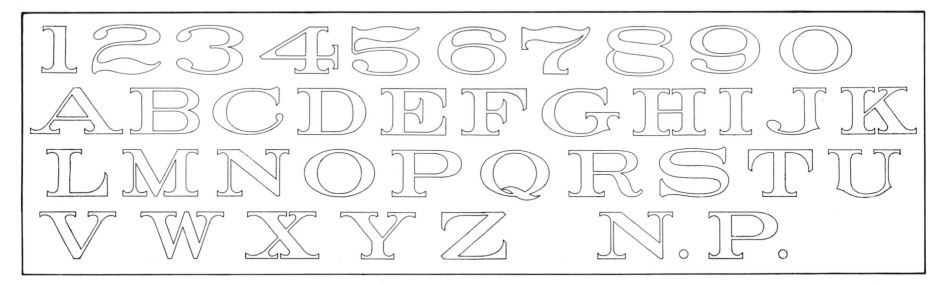

8" "Northern Pacific" stencil for tenders from NP drawing 21231-D of December 1939. The 'period' provides a puzzle as it was apparently applied at the prerogative or whim of the painter.

3" Class lettering for locomotives from NP drawing 21230 of May 1916.

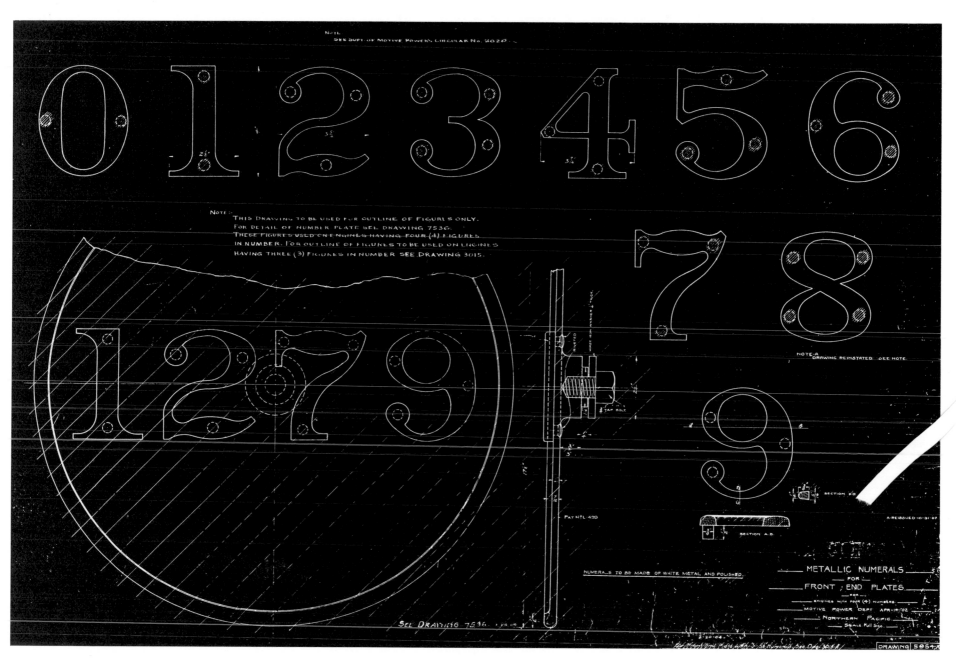

Metallic numerals for Front End Plates, NP drawing 5954-A, October 1907

M. I. MISSISSIPPI STREET
T. S. THIRD STREET
C. O. COMO
S. P. ST. PAUL
M. P. MINNEAPOLIS
M. T. MINN. TRANSFER
N. T. NORTHTOWN
D. U. DULUTH
S. U. SUPERIOR
B. D. BRAINERD
S. E. STAPLES
G. F. EAST GRAND FORKS
D. L. DILWORTH
J. T. JAMESTOWN
M. N. MANDAN
G. V. GLENDIVE
B. G. BILLINGS
L. R. LAUREL
L. V. LIVINGSTON
B. T. BUTTE
B. J. BEMIDJI

H. L. HELENA
M. S. MISSOULA
W. A. WALLACE
P. W. PARKWATER
S. K. SPOKANE
P. A. PASCO
Y. A. YAKIMA
L. T. LEWISTON
C. E. CLE ELUM
A. U. AUBURN
S. L. SEATTLE
K. S. KING STREET
T. A. TACOMA
S. T. SO. TACOMA
P. T. PORTLAND
B. M. BELLINGHAM
E. V. EVERETT
H. O. HOQUIAM

PAINTING & STENCILING
SHOP MARKS
NORTHERN PACIFIC RAILWAY CO.
MECHANICAL DEPT.   ST. PAUL. MINN.
AUG. 17, 1915   SCALE
APPROVED   CORRECT

GENERAL MECH. SUPT.   MECH. ENGR.
SERIES Y-1185   DRAWING 7189

Y
R.T.H
5·3·57

D.- G. H. W. 6-29-37
REDRAWN- R.T.H. 5-3-57
C.- R.A. 5-3-57

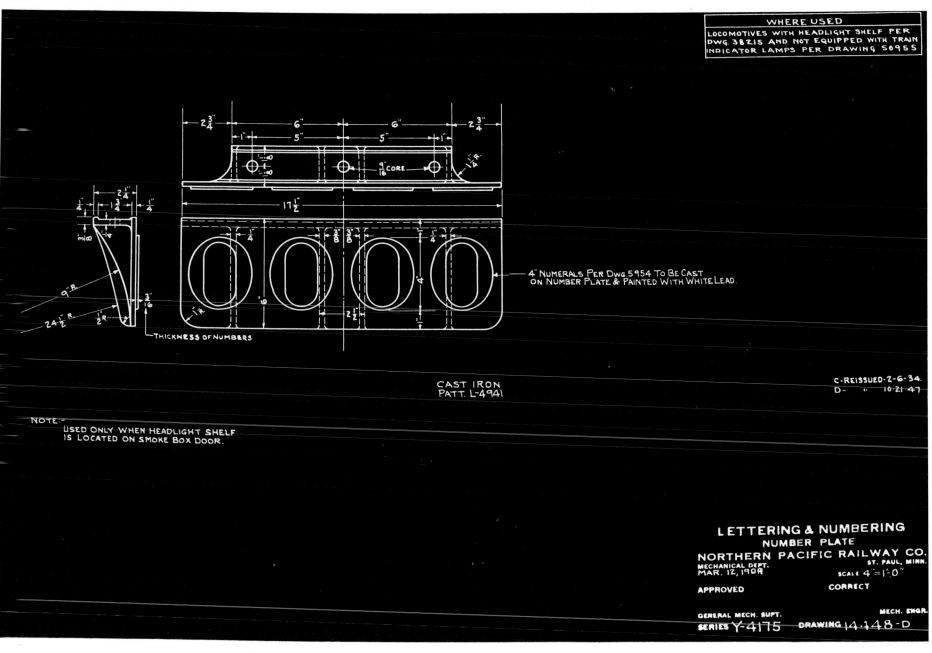

8" Locomotive number stencil from NP drawing 8973, March 1906.

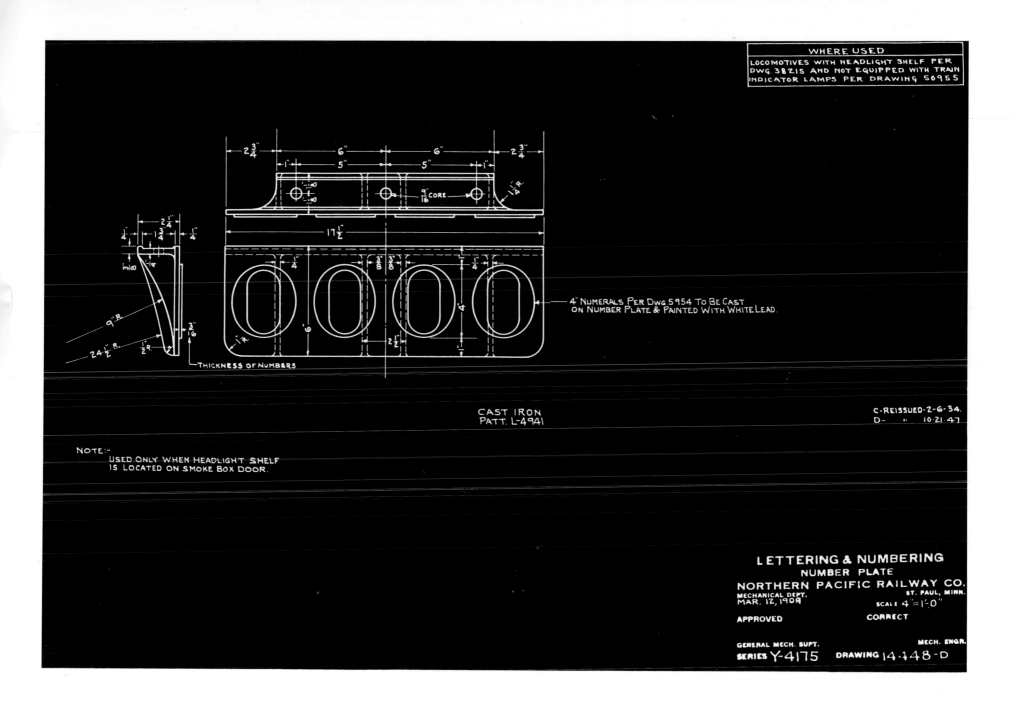

9" CORE

4" NUMERALS PER DWG. 5954 TO BE CAST
ON NUMBER PLATE & PAINTED WITH WHITE LEAD.

THICKNESS OF NUMBERS

CAST IRON
PATT. L-4941

C-REISSUED-2-6-34.
D- " 10-21-47

NOTE:-
USED ONLY WHEN HEADLIGHT SHELF
IS LOCATED ON SMOKE BOX DOOR.

LETTERING & NUMBERING
NUMBER PLATE
NORTHERN PACIFIC RAILWAY CO.
MECHANICAL DEPT.   ST. PAUL, MINN.
MAR. 12, 1909   SCALE 4"=1'-0"

APPROVED   CORRECT

GENERAL MECH. SUPT.   MECH. ENGR.
SERIES Y-4175   DRAWING 14.148-D

269

8" Locomotive number stencil from NP drawing 8973, March 1906.